PRI
THE

PRIDE OF
THE HEARTS

**The untold story of the men and women who made
the Great War heroes of Heart of Midlothian**

DEREK NIVEN

Corkerhill Press

Published in 2021 by Corkerhill Press

ISBN Paperback: 978-0-9935551-8-3
Ebook: 978-0-9935551-9-0

A CIP catalogue copy of this book can be found at the
British Library and at the National Library of Scotland.

Published with the help of Indie Authors World
www.indieauthorsworld.com

IndieAuthors
World

For my grandsons Cailean John Murphy
and Lewis Alan Murphy.

Acknowleᴅgments

The author wishes to acknowledge the valued assistance of Indie Authors World partners Sinclair and Kim Macleod in the publishing of this book. As always, I would like to thank Gillian Murphy for her expert editorial skills. A special thanks to my old railway colleagues John Steele and Robin Dale, who have both encouraged me to 'kick on' with the idea of the 'Pride' series.

Thanks to David Speed, the official Hearts historian, for his valued assistance, especially with research into the elusive Hearts hero Teddy McGuire, and also acknowledgment of the vast amount of background information on the Hearts players contained in the superb book *McCrae's Battalion* © Jack Alexander, 2003. My ASGRA colleague Margaret Hubble also provided excellent research into the West Lothian and Lancashire newspaper archives in connection with Teddy McGuire. Another ASGRA colleague, Bruce Bishop, a renowned expert in Elgin genealogy, helped with local research on Jamie Low.

Also to the late, great Sir Dirk Bogarde for the pseudonym and our shared alumni of Allan Glen's School.

Finally, without the unswerving love, support, and patience of my wife Linda, this 'Pride' series of books would never have seen the light of day.

The gaudy colouring with which she veiled her unhappiness
afforded as little real comfort as the gay uniform of the soldier
when it is drawn over his mortal wound.
– Sir Walter Scott, the Heart of Midlothian

The Old Lie: Dulce et decorum est, Pro patria mori.
- Wilfred Owen, WW1 poet

Contents

Preface

In this fourth book in the Pride series, the reader may again think this latest publication is about the beautiful game of football. On the contrary, it is more about fickle fate, destiny and the unflinching bravery, camaraderie and human spirit in the desperate heat of battle.

This book researches the chance accumulation of fateful meetings and unions between men and women from the early 19th century, which culminated in the procreation of a remarkable group of young men, who wrote themselves into the annals of history over a century ago. It is about men and women who were born more than half a century before the formation of a new association football club in 1874 in the district of Gorgie, in the city of Edinburgh, which eventually grew into the world-renowned Heart of Midlothian Football Club.

When the research on this book began in late 2019, the world was unaware it was to face the global COVID-19 pandemic, with predictions of up to 3 or 4 million lives lost. However, many lives are being saved by the ultra-fast developments of coronavirus vaccines in just 9 months. It will be recalled that when the surviving Hearts players returned from the Great War, the world was already in the throes of the 1918–19 Spanish Flu pandemic, which killed an estimated 50 million globally.

Hearts is the oldest football club in the Scottish capital of Edinburgh, founded by a group of friends from the Heart of Midlothian Quadrille Assembly, whose name was influenced by Walter Scott's novel The Heart of Midlothian, published in 1818. The modern club crest is based on the Heart of Midlothian cobbled mosaic on the city's Royal Mile outside St Giles Cathedral and the team's colours are predominantly maroon and white.

The early 19th century ancestors of the Hearts players were brought together by destiny, having no idea that one day their descendants would be immortalised. Not because they were intrinsically great Hearts footballers, although some were indeed exceptional players. It was because they enlisted en-masse during the Great War and so many of them paid the ultimate sacrifice for their King and country. For a more in-depth history of the Hearts players and their part in the 16th Battalion, the Royal Scots, the reader is recommended to read the enthralling and forensically researched book *McCrae's Battalion* © Jack Alexander, 2003.

The players and men of the Royal Scots are commemorated on the memorial clock-tower erected in the Haymarket Junction district of Edinburgh. It was unveiled on 9 April 1922, five years after the opening day of the dreadful Battle of Arras, where many men of the 16th Battalion fought and died. Secretary of State for Scotland, Robert Munro, told the attending crowd of 65,000 that the country owed a debt of gratitude to Hearts that could never be repaid.

The players are also commemorated on a memorial cairn at Contalmaison in the *Departement de la Somme* in northern France erected through funds raised by the Hearts Great War Committee. On 2 July 2016, on a soaking wet Saturday in France, exactly one hundred years after the second day of the dreadful Battle of the Somme, the author and his brother-in-law, Alex Scott, cycled up to Contalmaison. They arrived just in time to greet the Hearts committee and fans entering the church, L'église Saint-Léger, adjacent to the cairn for the centenary service of commemoration.

The previous day, on the 100th anniversary of the '*worst day in British military history*', when over 57,000 British and Allied soldiers were killed or injured, the author and his brother-in-law had attempted to cycle up to Gordon Cemetery at Mametz, not far from Contalmaison, where Alex's great-grandfather Private Francis Hepburn, 2nd Battalion Gordon Highlanders is buried. Frank Hepburn fell at Mametz Wood on that same first day of the Battle of the Somme that decimated the Hearts players at nearby Contalmaison. The author's visit was soon after the terrorist bombings in Belgium and Paris in 2016 and there was heightened security. The two intrepid cyclists failed to get past a French gendarmerie roadblock and were turned back on the ironic premise that: "*Angela Merkel was visiting the German cemetery at Fricourt.*"

This book also recognises that 2021 is the 100th anniversary of the formation of the Royal British Legion, who work tirelessly to honour the memory of those men and women who made the ultimate sacrifice.

Pride of the Hearts is not written from a footballing perspective, but continues the theme of honouring footballing heroes in Derek Niven's '*Pride Series*'. The author is, instead, a professional genealogist and member of the Association of Scottish Genealogists (ASGRA). The reader may ask what brought a professional genealogist to want to write the family history of the Hearts heroes of the Great War.

It was his support for Celtic, dating back to 1967, that kindled the idea for a series of books celebrating the family histories of famous Scottish footballing heroes. The first book in the series, published in 2017, is *Pride of the Lions*. The book celebrates the 50th anniversary of the Lisbon Lions, the first British team to lift the European Cup. It tackles this subject, not from a footballing perspective, but a genealogical, familial, religious, and social history perspective.

The second book in the series, published in 2018, is *Pride of the Jocks*. This book celebrates the 16 greatest Scottish football managers of the modern era, such as, Busby, Shankly, Stein, Ferguson, Souness, and Dalglish, again from the perspective of the men and women who created them in a genealogical sense.

The third publication, *Pride of the Bears*, celebrates the family histories of the men and women who were the progenitors of the Rangers team that won the European Cup Winners' Cup in 1972. Two of the medal winners for Rangers – Sandy Jardine and Alfie Conn – were also boyhood Hearts fans, going on to play for the Gorgie club later in their careers. Rangers captain John Greig was also a boyhood Hearts fan and had his eye set on Gorgie, but his father convinced him to sign for the Ibrox club. Alfie Conn's father,

Alfie Conn Senior, also played for Hearts and was one of the 'Terrible Trio' in the 1950s.

The 'Pride Series' serves to show, even in greatness, we are, as we say in Scotland, "a' Jock Tamson's bairns". The author's family history is a tale of poor, struggling agricultural labourers, coal miners, and railway workers striving to achieve more than their working-class existences afforded them. Within this history are tales of struggles through the Great War, tales of illegitimacy, infant mortality, and grinding poverty. The average reader will be able to associate their own family history in the same vein.

Likewise, the genealogy of the Hearts players reveals a remarkably similar story of mostly ordinary working-class boys from predominantly poor backgrounds who went on to achieve feats of extraordinary skill on the football field and outstanding bravery on the battlefield. The reader should be aware that it has not been possible to research every aspect of the lives of the ancestors of the Hearts players and, in the main, the detailed research concentrates on the Scottish family history of the 16 players who enlisted in 'McCrae's Battalion'.

In response to increasing appeals from the press, politicians and the public for volunteers, Lieutenant-Colonel Sir George McCrae MP, a popular figure in Edinburgh and a Hearts director, announced in November 1914 that he would raise his own battalion – the 16th Battalion, the Royal Scots – and he boasted it would be full within seven days. At that time, Hearts comfortably led the First Division, but 11 of their players, in addition to three players already serving, enlisted en-masse on 25 November 1914, with a further five being declared unfit to serve. The following day, a further two players signed up, bringing the total to 16 Hearts footballers enlisted in the battalion. 'McCrae's Battalion', as it came to be known, was the original 'sportsmen's battalion' in Kitchener's New Army.

At least 30 professional footballers enlisted, including players from Hibernian, Raith Rovers, Falkirk, and Dunfermline, as well as those from Hearts. Furthermore, players from the world of Scottish Junior football, rugby, and hockey also rallied to the cause. The battalion was to become the 16th Royal Scots, fondly known as McCrae's Battalion. The group of volunteers also contained some 500 Hearts fans and season ticket-holders, as well as 150 of their great Edinburgh rival Hibernian's supporters.

Pride of the Hearts.

This is their truly amazing story.

Chapter 1

Jimmy Boyd
Lance Corporal 18976,
16th Battalion Royal Scots

James Boyd (1894 – 1916)

James Boyd was born on 14 November 1894 at Seafield, Livingston, Linlithgowshire, to father James Boyd, a shale miner, and mother Jane Taket Renwick. The birth was registered by his father James Boyd on 29 November 1894 at the Livingston Registry Office. The family later lived and worked at Mossend, West Calder, Midlothian and Jimmy started his football career with the Mossend Swifts, known as the 'cow-punchers'. Jimmy, a printer working in West Calder, became a professional footballer playing for Heart of Midlothian from early 1914, alongside his goalkeeper brother, Archibald Renwick Boyd. Hearts' boss John McCartney recorded in the press, citing one of Hearts greatest players, *"Young Boyd puts me in mind of Bobby Walker. We will give him a chance and see if he makes the grade."*

At the outbreak of the Great War, Archie and Jimmy, both keen to enlist, returned to their parents' home in Mossend, West Calder. Archie was engaged to be married and Jimmy was single, so the family came to a heart-breaking and fateful decision: Jimmy would sign up. Jimmy Boyd enlisted in November 1914, alongside Pat Crossan, as a

Private in McCrae's Battalion for service in the Great War. In June 1915 the 16th was transferred for basic training to Studley Royal Camp, Ripon, Yorkshire, and came under the command of 101st Brigade, 34th Division. The battalion moved on to Sutton Veny, Wiltshire in September 1915 and made final preparations to sail for France and the Western Front.

The 16th, including Jimmy, landed at Le Havre on 8 January 1916. The battalion's first action was at Contalmaison on 1 July 1916, at the outset of the Battle of the Somme. The battalion took part in the initial assault that first day on the right flank of the British attack. In doing so they were the only part of the 34th Division, and virtually in the whole of the British offensive, to achieve their initial object-ive, yet had advanced less than two kilometres towards the village of La Boisselle. Sir George McCrae was in the thick of battle alongside his men and was awarded the DSO for Gallantry. They were relieved on 3 July, with Sir George being the last man back, and they went into a rest area until 30 July when, with their casualties replaced, they returned to the front-line in the Mametz and High Wood area.

On the night of 30 July, the 16th and the Suffolks mounted an assault on the German-held Intermediate Trench at Bazentin-le-Petit. Four days later, Jimmy was seriously injured in his side by a piece of shell casing. A stretcher-party was brought up under intense shelling and they set off with Jimmy for the dressing station south of Bazentin. None of the group ever made it back and Jimmy was posted missing. Annan Ness wrote to McCartney stating Jimmy had almost certainly been killed.

Lance Corporal James Boyd, 21, died on 3 August 1916, one month into the dreadful Somme battle, that went on to claim a half a million casualties. In the Service Returns for August, Jimmy was recorded as 'presumed dead'. Pat Crossan, recovering from wounds in Stourbridge Hospital, received a letter from John McCartney that Jimmy's body had been found and buried near Bazentin. The battlefield graveyard was later destroyed in the to and fro of trench warfare and Jimmy's body was never recovered. He is commemorated on the Thiepval Memorial, on Pier and Faces 6D and 7D, and also on the Commonwealth War Graves Commission (CWGC) website, as the son of James and Jane Boyd of 50 Front Street, Mossend, West Calder, Midlothian. Private 18976 James Boyd was posthumously awarded the Victory and British War medals.

Twelve days after Jimmy's death, the 16th was relieved on 15 August when 34th Division moved out of the Somme sector, although the battle raged on until 1 November 1916. Colonel Sir George McCrae, the hero of Contalmaison, received unfair criticism from General Nicholson for the failure to capture the Intermediate Trench, and by November, McCrae was broken by the battalion's losses on the Somme and by exhaustion. He was posted home but the battalion proudly remained 'McCrae's Own'.

Jimmy's parents - James Boyd and
Jane Taket Renwick

Jimmy's father James Boyd was born on 7 January 1864 at Strain's Land, Whifflet, Old Monkland, Lanarkshire, to father William Boyd, a miner, and mother Susan Waddell. The birth was registered by his father William Boyd, who signed with his 'x' mark, on 27 January 1864 at the Old Monkland Registry Office. Jimmy's mother Jane Taket Renwick, aka Jeanie, was born on 22 December 1865 in Blackburn, Livingston, Linlithgowshire, to father Archibald Renwick, a labourer, and mother Jane White McAulay. The birth was registered by her father Archibald Renwick on 11 January 1866 at the Livingston Registry Office.

Jane's father Archibald was dead before 1871. In 1871, Jane Renwick, 5, resided at Polbeath Farm, West Calder, with her stepfather John McPherson, 38, a labourer, mother Jane, 35, and her siblings.

In 1881, James, 17, a coal miner, resided at 53 Front Street, Mossend, West Calder, with his father William Boyd, 38, a widowed coal miner, and his siblings. Boyd became a shale miner like his father before him, a major industry in the Linlithgowshire and West Lothian area at that time. The shale was mined manually and then processed to extract the shale oil within the rock. Nowadays, the process used to extract shale oil is called fracking, although, currently there is a moratorium on its use in Scotland.

James Boyd, 21, a shale miner, of 34 Front Street, Mossend, West Calder, married Jane Taket Renwick, 19, a domestic servant, of West Calder, on 27 March 1885 at

James's family home. The wedding was conducted by Rev Donald Taylor, minister of West Calder Free Church; the best man was Robert Boyd, James's brother, and the best maid was Maggie Renwick, Jane's cousin. James and Jane had four known children; in West Calder, Jeanie (b. ~1885), Susan (b. ~1887), Archibald (b. ~1890), and at Seafield, Livingston, James (b. 14 November 1894).

In 1891, James Boyd, 29, a shale miner, resided at 49 Front Street, Mossend, West Calder, with wife Jane, 25, Jeanie, 6, Susan, 4, both scholars, and Archibald, 11 months old. James and Jane were still alive and living at 50 Front Street, Mossend, West Calder, in August 1916 when their son Jimmy was killed near Mametz during the Battle of the Somme.

Jimmy's paternal grandparents – William Boyd and Susan Waddell

Jimmy's paternal grandfather William Boyd was born around 1843 in Old Monkland, Lanarkshire to father James Boyd, a mines overseer, and mother Margaret Graham. His grandmother Susan Waddell was born around 1840 in Old Monkland to father James Waddell, a gamekeeper, and mother Keir Ewan. William Boyd, 21, a miner, married Susan Waddell, 20, both residing in Whifflet, Old Monkland, on 13 December 1861 at the Manse. The wedding was conducted by Rev John Johnston, minister of Old Monkland Church of Scotland; the best man was John Boyd, William's brother, and the best maid was Catherine Boyd, William's sister.

William and Susan had six known children; in Whifflet, James (b. 7 January 1864) and Robert (b. ~1867), in West Calder, Mary (b. ~1869), Helen (b. ~1871), Janet (b. ~1874) and Jane (b. ~1880). Shortly after the birth of daughter Jane, Susan Boyd nee Waddell, 41, died on 18 July 1880 at 1 North Row, Summerlee, Coatbridge of chronic diarrhoea and acute bronchitis as certified by Dr William S Donald MB CM. William travelled from the family home in Mossend, West Calder to register his wife's death on 19 July 1880 at the Coatbridge Registry Office. The district of Summerlee was at the heart of Coatbridge's coal mining and iron and steel industries. Summerlee has been preserved as an Industrial Heritage Park and Museum.

In 1881, William Boyd, 38, a widowed coal miner, resided at 53 Front Street, Mossend, West Calder, with children James, 17, Robert, 14, both coal miners, Mary, 12, at home, Helen, 9, and Janet, 7, both scholars, and Jane, 1. William Boyd, a shale miner, was still alive in 1885 and living in West Calder.

Jimmy's maternal grandparents –
Archibald Renwick and Jane White McAulay

Jimmy's maternal grandfather Archibald Renwick was born on 4 November 1819 at Strathaven, Avondale, Lanarkshire, to father Archibald Renwick, a farmer, and mother Jane Tackit. The birth is recorded in the OPRs for the Strathaven Associate Session church (Ref: CH3/289/2/222) as follows:-

1819: Archibald lawful son to Archibald Renwick born on November the 4th and baptized on the 21st November 1819

Strathaven Associate Session was formed in 1738 as part of the Associate Presbytery and a church was built around 1764, with a new church erected the year after Archibald's birth in 1820, later becoming part of the United Presbyterian Church of Scotland.

Jimmy's maternal grandmother Jane White McAulay was born around 1835 at Whitburn, Linlithgowshire, to father John McAulay, a pithead man, and mother Margaret Forrester. Archibald Renwick, 37, a ploughman, of Whitburn, Linlithgowshire, married Jane McAulay, 23, a domestic servant, of Longridge, Linlithgowshire, on 17 December 1858. The wedding was conducted by Rev James Ronaldson, minister of Longridge United Presbyterian Church; the witnesses were George Forrester and Edward Roberts.

Archibald and Jane had three known children; Archibald (b. ~1860, Corstorphine), Jane (b. 22 December 1865, Blackburn), and John (b. ~1868, West Calder). In 1861, Archibald Renwick, 39, a chemical works labourer, resided in the village of Whitburn, with wife Jane, 25, and son Archibald, 1. Archibald worked at the nearby Bathgate Chemical Works, an extensive factory used to manufacture paraffin oil and naphthalene from coal gas raised from the shale mines in its immediate vicinity. The property was owned by Durham Weir Esquire and occupied by Messrs. Meldrum and Young, chemists, Bathgate.

Archibald Renwick, 50, a farm servant, of Polbeath Farm, met an unfortunate end, when on 30 December 1869, '*he sustained injuries received from a train on a railway having passed over him and crushed him*'. Archibald died eight days later on 7 January 1870 at his home at Coalbytte, West Calder, as certified by Robert L Stuart, Procurator Fiscal on 1 February 1870 in a Register of Corrected Entries.

With three young children to raise, Jane soon remarried her second husband John McPherson, a labourer. In 1871, Jane, 35, resided at Polbeath Farm, West Calder, with husband John McPherson, 38, a labourer, children Archibald Renwick, 11, Jane Renwick, 5, John Renwick, 3, and baby Janet McPherson, 8 days old. Also, lodging at Polbeath Farm was Francis Craig, 40, a farm servant, and Alexander Deans, 25, a miner. Jane McPherson previously Renwick nee McAulay was still alive in 1885.

Jimmy's paternal great-grandparents
James Boyd and Margaret Graham

Jimmy's paternal great-grandfather James Boyd was born around 1800 in New Monkland and his great-grandmother Margaret Graham was born around 1805 in Old Monkland, Lanarkshire. James Boyd married Margaret Graham in Airdrie, New Monkland on 28 October 1827 and paid 3/6d to the Church of Scotland Poor Fund. This lent credence to the old joke, "*Three and six – was she worth it?*"The marriage is recorded in the OPRs for Airdrie or New Monkland (Ref: 651/7/98) as follows:-

1827: 4th Sabbath: James Boyd in this Parish and
Margaret Graham in the Parish of Old Monkland: 3s 6d

James and Margaret had three known children; William (b. ~1840, Old Monkland), John, and Catherine. James, a mine's overseer, was still alive in 1861, although, wife Margaret was dead by then.

Jimmy's paternal great-grandparents
James Waddell and Keir Ewan

Jimmy's other paternal great-grandfather James Waddell and his great-grandmother Keir Ewan were born around 1810 probably in Lanarkshire. James, a gamekeeper, married wife Keir and they had a known daughter Susan (b. ~1840) in Old Monkland. James, a gamekeeper, and wife Keir were both still alive in 1861.

Jimmy's maternal great-grandparents
Archibald Renwick and Jane Tackit

Jimmy's maternal great-grandfather Archibald Renwick and his great-grandmother Jane Tackit (or Taket) were born around 1795 probably in Avondale, Lanarkshire. Archibald and Jane had a known son Archibald (b. 4 November 1819) in Strathaven. Archibald Renwick, a farmer, was dead by 1858 and his wife Jane was dead by 1870.

Jimmy's maternal great-grandparents
John McAulay and Margaret Forrester

Jimmy's other maternal great-grandfather John McAulay and his great-grandmother Margaret Forrester were born around 1810 probably in Whitburn, Linlithgowshire, now in West Lothian. John and Margaret had a known daughter Jane (b. ~1835, Whitburn). John, a pithead man, and Margaret were both still alive in 1858. John was still alive in Whitburn in January 1870, when he registered the death of his son-in-law Archibald Renwick.

Chapter 2

Duncan Currie
Sergeant 18999,
16th Battalion Royal Scots

Duncan Currie (1892 – 1916)

D uncan Currie was born on 13 August 1892 at 18 Double Row, Eglinton Ironworks, Kilwinning, Ayrshire, to father Robert Currie, a coal miner, and mother Mary Ann Percy. After schooling, Duncan became an assistant hairdresser working for his brother in Kilwinning, but fate was drawing him towards a career in professional football in Edinburgh. In 1911, Duncan, 18, an assistant hairdresser, resided at 83 Main Street, Kilwinning, with his father Robert Currie, 56, a roads-man in the mine, mother Mary, 56, and his other siblings. Around 1912, he started his career playing for junior side Kilwinning Rangers, a team that was openly supported by the wealthy Baird family, owners of Eglinton Ironworks. Duncan's father Robert was a Baird's employee.

At one time William Baird & Company's Eglinton Iron Works produced 25% of Scotland's pig iron. Education was considered essential in instilling the employers' values in their community, with a particular focus on religious studies. Bairds used the mediums of sport, recreation, and education to build a sense of solidarity amongst their workforce. The firm built workers' institutes at Kilwinning, Lugar, Muirkirk, Gartsherrie, and Twechar.

Bairds also gave their patronage to junior football clubs like Kilwinning Rangers and Larkhall Thistle. If social control was the aim of this sporting patronage, it is impossible to analyse its relative 'successes' in forcing local footballers to accept the moral perspective of their patrons. Footballers and supporters in these communities were pre-disposed to support Protestant organisations, such as Rangers. As Catholics faced discrimination from Protestant workplaces and cultural spheres, it was logical that they too would gravitate towards Catholic associations, such as Celtic.

Duncan became a professional footballer with Hearts, initially as a left-winger, and then at full-back, between 1912 and 1915, making 45 appearances. His honours as a Hearts player include: 1912–13 North Eastern Cup, 1913–14 East of Scotland Shield, 1913–14 Rosebery Charity Cup, and 1914–15 Wilson Cup.

Duncan's brothers Bob and Sam also played professional football. Robert Currie was a forward, best remembered during his five years with Bury. Bob started as an amateur with Galston, then he moved to Kilwinning Eglinton. He also played for Hearts, Arthurlie, Abercorn and Morton. He won the North Eastern Cup in 1912–13 with Hearts alongside Duncan. Samuel Percy Currie made over 230 appearances for Leicester City as a full-back and captained the club. Sam began his career with his hometown junior club Kilwinning Rangers, with whom he won the 1908–09 Scottish Junior Cup.

On 25 November 1914, along with his Hearts team-mates, Duncan enlisted at the Royal Scots recruiting office in Edinburgh in McCrae's Battalion and he was promoted to Sergeant. On 30 June 1916, the night before the Big Push, most of the 16th spent time scribbling in pencil on Page 12 of their Pay Books, their 'Soldier's Short Form of Will'. As fate would have it, Currie wrote to his father, stating outright that he would not make out a will as he did not require one.

At 7.30am on 1 July, Currie along with C Company went over the top into No Man's Land attacking the German front line at La Boisselle. By mid-morning and some miracle, while the other companies of the 16th were being decimated, C Company, led by Captain Lionel Coles, remained fairly intact and was making steady progress. Coles, with C Company and a few stragglers from other units, decided to try and make another charge to reach the village. They emerged from the sunken road leading up to La Boisselle to find three or four German machine-guns trained on them. Hearts men were falling like ninepins. Annan Ness saw Duncan Currie hit in the right shoulder and he also witnessed Harry Wattie go down.

Sergeant 18999 Duncan Currie, 23, was killed in action near La Boisselle on 1 July 1916, on that horrendous first day of the Battle of the Somme, when British and Allied soldiers sustained 57,000 casualties, including 11,000 killed, and which became known as the 'worst day in British military history'.

Currie, Captain Coles, and Peter Ross were buried in a battlefield plot on the La Boisselle–Contalmaison Road, but the cemetery was later destroyed. Duncan Currie is commemorated on the Thiepval Memorial, on the same Pier and Faces 6D and 7D as his Hearts pal Jimmy Boyd, and also on the CWGC website. Sergeant 18999 Duncan Currie was posthumously awarded the Victory and British War medals.

Duncan's parents - Robert Currie and Mary Ann Percy

Duncan's father Robert Currie was born on 22 February 1855 in Barrachnie, Old Monkland, Lanarkshire, to father Robert Currie, a coal miner, and mother Jane Paterson. The birth was registered by his father Robert Currie, a collier, on 24 February 1855 at the Baillieston Registry Office. Duncan's mother Mary Ann Percy was born around January 1855 in Kilwinning, Ayrshire to father Robert Percy, a furnaceman, and mother Catherine Kelly. The birth is recorded in the CPRs for St Mary's RC, Saltcoats as follows:-

> *Maryanne (Mixed): Lawful: Robert Percy and Catherine Kelley: 4 months [old]: [Baptism] 12th May 1855: [Sponsor] Ally Connahan: [Priest] William Hallinan*

In 1861, Mary Ann, 6, resided at 22 Single Row, Eglinton Ironworks, Kilwinning, with her father Robert Percy, 35, an iron furnace filler, mother Catherine, 36, and her other siblings.

Robert Currie, 18, a coal miner, of Byrehill Row, Kilwinning, married wife Mary Ann Percy, 18, a millworker, of Eglinton Ironworks, Kilwinning, both signing with their 'x' marks, on 4 July 1873 at Eglinton Ironworks. The wedding was conducted by Rev William Lee Ker, minister of Kilwinning parish; the best man was James Percy, Robert's brother, and the best maid was Isabel Percy, Robert's sister.

Robert and Mary Ann had 11 known children in Kilwinning, although only 8 survived into adulthood, including; James (b. <1879), Isabel, aka Bella (b. ~1880), Alexander (b. ~1883), Catherine, aka Kate (b. ~1891) and Duncan (b. 13 August 1892). Son Duncan Currie was born on 13 August 1892 at 18 Double Row, Eglinton Ironworks, Kilwinning, to father Robert Currie, a coal miner, and mother Mary Ann Percy. The family still lived in Double Row in 1898, when Robert registered his father's death. In 1911, Robert Currie, 56, a roads-man in the mine, resided at 83 Main Street, Kilwinning, with wife Mary Ann, 56, children Bella, 31, Alexander, 28, a hairdresser on his own account, Kate, 20, a mill girl in a spinning mill, and Duncan, 18, an assistant hairdresser.

Duncan's paternal grandparents -
Robert Currie and Jane Paterson

Duncan's paternal grandfather Robert Currie was born around 1826 in Barrachnie, Old Monkland, to father Campbell Currie and mother Margaret Fleming. Duncan's grandmother Jane Paterson was born illegitimately around 1825 in Baillieston, Old Monkland, to reputed father Alexander Paterson, and mother Agnes Hutchison. In 1841, Robert, 15, a labourer, resided in Barrachnie, Old Monkland, with his father Campbell Currie, 40, a labourer, mother Margaret, 45, a tambourer, and his other siblings.

Robert Currie, a collier, married wife Jane Paterson in 1846 in Glasgow, Lanarkshire and they had six known children; in Old Monkland, Alexander (b. ~1850), Agnes (b.

~1853), Robert (b. 22 February 1855), in Kilwinning, Duncan (b. ~1858), Margaret (b. ~1860) and Jane (b. ~1863). Son Robert Currie was born on 22 February 1855 in Barrachnie, Old Monkland, Lanarkshire, to father Robert Currie, a coal miner, and mother Jane Paterson, however, by 1858 the family had moved to Kilwinning in Ayrshire.

Jane Currie nee Paterson, 40, died on 8 January 1865 at 43 Byrehill Row, Kilwinning of kidney disease as certified by David D Service MD, surgeon. In 1871, Robert Currie, 46, a widowed coal miner, still resided at 43 Byrehill Row, Kilwinning, with children Alexander, 21, Robert, 16, Duncan, 13, all coal miners, Margaret, 11, and Jane, 8, both scholars. Also residing with Robert was his son-in-law John Hislop, 25, a coal miner, daughter Agnes Hislop, 18, and grandson John Hislop, 10 months old.

In 1881, Robert Currie, 56, a coal miner, resided at No.20 Byrehill Row, Kilwinning, with daughters Margaret, 21, an unemployed farm servant, and Jane, 19, a field labourer. In 1891, Robert, 66, a riddler in a coal mine, still resided at 20 Byrehill Row, with Irish son-in-law Thomas Hampton, 31, a coal pit stone contractor, daughter Jane Hampton, 28, grandchildren Jane, 8, John, 6, Elizabeth, 4, and Robert, 2. Robert Currie, stated as 67, died at 20 Barrel [Byrehill] Row, Kilwinning on 7 June 1898 of apoplexy of the brain as certified by Dr A Milroy MD. The death was registered by his son Robert Currie, of 18 Double Row, Eglinton Ironworks, Kilwinning, on 7 June 1898 at the Kilwinning Registry Office.

Duncan's maternal grandparents - Robert Percy and Catherine Kelly

Duncan's maternal grandfather Robert Percy was born about 1826 and his grandmother Catherine Kelly was born about 1825, both in Ireland. Robert, an Ulster Protestant, and Catherine, a Catholic, married in Ireland around 1850, during the period of the Irish Potato Famine (1846–52) and they had six known children; in Ireland, Jane (b. ~1852), James (b. ~1854), in Kilwinning, Mary Ann (b. January 1855), Isabella (b. ~1857), Robert (b. ~1858) and William (b. ~1860). The family moved to Kilwinning around 1855 and Robert got a job as a furnaceman in Baird's Eglinton Ironworks. At that time, Baird's advertised in Belfast newspapers, openly seeking workers of mainly Protestant backgrounds.

In 1861, Robert Percy, 35, an iron furnace filler, resided at 22 Single Row, Eglinton Ironworks, Kilwinning, with wife Catherine, 36, children Jane, 9, James, 7, Mary Ann, 6, all scholars, Isabella, 4, Robert, 3, and William, 1. Also lodging at Robert's home was Irish-born Thomas McMenamy, 18, a coal pit bottomer. Robert Percy, a furnaceman, was still alive in 1873, although his wife Catherine was dead by then.

Duncan's paternal great-grandparents - Campbell Currie and Margaret Fleming

Duncan's paternal great-grandfather Campbell Currie was born around 1799 and his grandmother Margaret Fleming was born around 1796 both in Old Monkland, Lanarkshire.

Campbell married Margaret and they had five known children in Barrachnie, Old Monkland; Robert (b. ~1826), Jean (b. ~1827), Margaret (b. ~1829), Charles (b. ~1831) and Christina (b. ~1833). In 1841, Campbell Currie, 40, a labourer, resided in Barrachnie, Old Monkland, in the quoad sacra parish of Crosshill, with wife Margaret, 45, a tambourer, Robert, 15, a labourer, Jean, 14, and Margaret, 12, both tambourers, Charles, 10, and Christina, 8. Living next door was Agness Fleming, 40, most likely Margaret's sister. A tambourer was a sewer who embroidered intricate patterns on to linen and cotton, using a round tambour to stretch the cloth. The tambourine percussion instrument was developed using a similar technique.

Duncan's paternal great-grandparents – Alexander Paterson and Agnes Hutchison

Duncan's other paternal great-grandfather Alexander Paterson and great-grandmother Agnes Hutchison were both born around 1800 probably in Lanarkshire. Alexander Paterson, the father of repute, and Agnes Hutchison had a daughter Jane Paterson born illegitimately around 1825 in Baillieston, Old Monkland. Alexander and Agnes never married each other. Alexander Paterson, a coal miner, and Agnes McDonald nee Hutchison, by then married, were both still alive in 1865.

Chapter 3

Ernest Edgar Ellis
Private 19009,
16th Battalion Royal Scots

Ernest Edgar Ellis (1885 – 1916)

Ernest Edgar Ellis was born on 30 November 1885 in the village of Sprowston, near Norwich, Norfolk, England, to father Henry William Ellis, a bootmaker, and mother Marie Taylor. After leaving school Ernie became a machine operator in a boot-making factory, however, he dreamt of becoming a professional footballer. In 1903, he began his career playing at right-back as an amateur for Thorpe Village and Norwich St James, and then he was signed professionally by Norwich City on 30 August 1907. In season 1908–09 he made 29 appearances for Doncaster Rovers, before transferring to Barnsley from 1909–10, where he made four appearances. In 1911, Ernest Edgar Ellis, 25, a professional footballer, resided at East Wymer, Norwich, with his father Harry William Ellis, 57, a bootmaker, mother Maria, 57, and his other siblings.

He then moved to Hartlepool United and from 1912–14 he played right-back in 74 games, before being transferred to Hearts, where he joined the Maroons on their successful summer tour of Denmark. Ellis managed just one appearance for Hearts and, when the Great War erupted, he joined the band of Hearts players who marched down on 25 November 1914 to recruit in McCrae's Battalion.

After enlisting in the Royal Scots he married his sweetheart, Isabella Armstrong, daughter of Thomas Armstrong, a railway signalman, and Catherine Bigman. Ernest Edgar Ellis, 26, a professional footballer and Private 16th Royal Scots, lodging with his in-laws at 191 Gorgie Road, and based at Studley Royal Camp, Ripon, married Isabella McRae Armstrong, 18, a clerk, also of 191 Gorgie Road, Gorgie, Edinburgh, on 29 July 1915 at 90 Craighouse Road, Edinburgh. The wedding was conducted by Rev J Bell Nicoll, minister of the Church of Scotland; the best man was Ernie's pal William Rose Wilson, another Hearts player in McCrae's, and the best maid was Helen Scott Armstrong, Isabella's sister.

Ernie and Isabella had very little time to spend together and he soon had to return to Studley Royal Camp in Ripon. By September 1915 the battalion transferred to Sutton Veny Camp, Wiltshire in preparation for transfer to France in early 1916. The likelihood is that Ernest and Isabella never saw each other again after that, as the battalion prepared for the summer offensive on the Somme battlefield. However, Isabella had fallen pregnant and Ernie became a father while he was stationed in France. Daughter Catherine Marie Ellis, aka Kitty, was born on 11 February 1916 at 191 Gorgie Road, Edinburgh. Ellis was never to see or hold his daughter.

On that terrible first day on the Somme, 1 July 1916, the same day that his teammate Duncan Currie fell, Ellis went over the top near Contalmaison, the 16th's primary objective. He was killed by sustained machine-gun fire in front of the

German frontline trench in an attack on the French village of La Boisselle, just yards away from his friends Currie and Wattie. Contalmaison is forever etched into the hearts and minds of Heart of Midlothian's club and fans.

On 16 September 1916, as the Somme raged on, Annan Ness received a letter from John McCartney stating that Ellis's remains had been found near Contalmaison and his teenage widow Isabella was anxious to visit the grave. Ness wrote to Isabella politely deterring her from visiting France, which reflected a growing ignorance at home about the indescribable conditions on the Western Front. Ellis's battlefield grave was later destroyed and he is commemorated on the Thiepval Memorial, on the same Pier and Faces 6D and 7D as his Hearts pals Jimmy Boyd and Duncan Currie. He is also commemorated on the CWGC website, as the son of Harry and Marie Ellis, of 236 Sprowston Road, Norwich and husband of Isobel Ellis, of 25 Tarvit Street, Edinburgh. Private 19009 Ernest Edgar Ellis was posthumously awarded the Victory and British War medals.

Ernie's parents –
Henry William Ellis and Maria Christina Taylor

Ernie's father Henry William Ellis, aka Harry, was born in 3rd Quarter 1853 in St Pancras, London, Middlesex to father Robert Ellis, a master shoemaker, and mother Maria Emma Waite. After leaving school Harry went into his father's shoe manufacturing business and by 1870 the family had moved to

Sprowston, Norfolk. Ernie's mother Maria Christina Taylor, aka Marie, was born in 1st Quarter 1855 in Norwich, Norfolk.

In 1871, Harry W, 17, a shoe riveter, resided in Sprowston, Norfolk, with his father Robert Ellis, 46, a shoe manufacturer, mother Maria E, 42, and his other siblings. Harry William Ellis married Maria Taylor in 1st Quarter 1878 as registered in Volume 4b and Page 214 in the Norwich Registry Office. Harry and Maria had five known children in Sprowston; Norah May (b. 17 March 1879), Harry William (b. ~1881), Ernest Edgar (b. 30 November 1885), Ivy Elsie (b. ~1889) and Sydney Lance (b. ~1895).

In 1881, Harry W Ellis, 27, a bootmaker, resided at Main Road, Sprowston, near Norwich, Norfolk, with wife Maria, 26, daughter Norah May, 2, and baby son Harry William. Son Ernest Edgar Ellis was born on 30 November 1885 in Sprowston, near Norwich, Norfolk.

In 1901, Harry Ellis, 47, a boot-laster, resided at Sprowston, Norwich, with wife Maria, 46, and son Harry, 20, a boot clicker. In 1911, Harry William Ellis, 57, a bootmaker, resided at East Wymer, Norwich, with wife Maria, 57, children Ernest Edgar, 25, a professional footballer, Ivy Elsie, 22, a bookbinder's assistant, and Sydney Lance, 16, a shoe and leather binding clerk. Harry William Ellis, a bootmaker, and his wife Maria were both living at 236 Sprowston Road, Norwich in July 1916, when son Ernie was killed at the Battle of the Somme.

Ernie's paternal grandparents –
Robert Ellis and Maria Emma Waite

Ernie's paternal grandfather Robert Ellis was born around 1825 in Northwold, Norfolk to father Samuel Ellis, a shoemaker, and mother Susan Reynolds and baptized on 23 January 1825 in Northwold St Andrew's Church of England as recorded in the Norfolk Bishop's Transcripts as follows:-

1825: Publickly January 23rd: No.406: Robert son of: Samuel Ellis and Susan Reynolds: Northwold: [Occupation] Shoemaker: W C Leach Curate

Ernie's grandmother Maria Emma Waite was born around 1829 in St James, London, Middlesex.

In 1841, the Ellis family were in dire straits and Robert, 15, lived the existence of a real-life Oliver Twist, residing in the St Pancras Workhouse, Augustus Street, St Pancras, London, with his father Samuel Ellis, 35, mother Susan, 35, and his other siblings. However, Robert was determined to escape the deprivations of the workhouse and improve his lot in life.

Robert Ellis, a shoemaker, married Maria Emma Waite in 3rd Quarter 1849 in Clerkenwell, London, Middlesex, as registered in Volume 3 page 103 of the Clerkenwell Registry Office. Robert and Maria had nine known children in London; Robert Hayes (b. ~1850, died in infancy), Henry William, aka Harry (b. 3rd Quarter 1853), Robert (b. ~1857), Horace (b, ~1859), Helen (b. ~1861), Sydney H (b. ~1863), Eva Rebecca (b. ~1865), Walter J (b. ~1867) and Ethel F (b. ~1870, possibly died in infancy). In 1851, Robert Ellis, 26, a master shoemaker, resided in Marylebone Lane,

Marylebone, London, with wife Maria Emma, 22, and son Robert Hayes, 1.

In the 1760s, Marylebone Lane was still a country lane on the fringes of the fast expanding city of London, which meandered along the edge of the River Tyburn. By the 1850s the lane was a bustling street full of shops and businesses, like Robert's boot and shoe shop. It is now a major shopping street to the north of Oxford Street and although the Tyburn has long been culverted underground, the lane still retains its winding river origins.

Son Henry William Ellis, aka Harry, was born in 3rd Quarter 1853 in St Pancras, London, Middlesex. By 1871, Robert had returned to his birthplace of Norfolk and started up his own shoe manufacturing business. At that time Norwich was fast becoming a centre of boot and shoe-making, later spawning large manufacturers such as Saxone's and Startrite. By the 1930s over 10,000 workers were employed in the Norwich shoe manufactories.

In 1871, Robert Ellis, 46, a shoe manufacturer, resided in Sprowston, Norfolk, with wife Maria E, 42, children Harry W, 17, a shoe riveter, Robert, 14, Horace, 12, Helen, 10, Sydney H, 8, Eva R, 6, all five scholars, Walter J, 4, and Ethel F, 1. By 1881, Robert and Maria had returned to live and work in Paddington, London, taking the two surviving youngest of their children, Walter and Eva. The older children, with Harry W Ellis, the head of household, remained to live and work in Sprowston in the shoe industry. Robert and Maria remained in Paddington for the rest of their lives and Maria died there in 1893.

Ernie's paternal great-grandparents –
Samuel Ellis and Susan Reynolds

Ernie's paternal great-grandfather Samuel Ellis, son of a boot-maker, was born around 1805 in Swaffham, Norfolk, and his great-grandmother Susan Reynolds was born around 1803 in Cockley Cley, Norfolk, lying a few miles south of Swaffham. Samuel Ellis was the older brother of John Ellis (1810–1890). Born in Swaffham, Norfolk in 1810, John Ellis, son of a boot-maker, was perhaps the most prominent member of the Ellis family, through his work with the rehabilitation of young criminals, leading him to help in the foundation of Reformatory Schools. John Ellis had been helping teach young boys shoemaking skills at the Ragged School in Brook Street, London and Charles Adderley MP, later Lord Norton, was so impressed, he made Ellis the first superintendent of his new Birmingham Reformatory School in 1852.

Samuel Ellis, a shoemaker, married Susan Reynolds around 1824 and they had four known children; in Norfolk, Robert (b. ~1825), Samuel (b. ~1829), Elizabeth (b. ~1831), and in St Pancras, London, William (b. ~1833). Son Robert was born around 1825 in Northwold, Norfolk to father Samuel Ellis, a shoemaker, and mother Susan Reynolds and baptized on 23 January 1825 in Northwold St Andrew's Church of England.

After the end of the Napoleonic Wars in 1815, there was growing unrest, particularly in rural economies such as Norfolk and the 1820s saw sustained periods of unemployment, depression and failed harvests. The proscriptive Corn Laws were having a terrible effect on the poor, keeping the price of bread artificially high. By the early 1830s the Ellis family were in dire straits and decided to move to London. They ended up in that most Dickensian of pauper institutions, the Victorian Workhouse.

In 1841, Samuel Ellis, 35, resided in the St Pancras Workhouse, Augustus Street, St Pancras, London, with wife Susan, 35, children Robert, 15, Samuel, 12, Elizabeth 10, and William, 8. In 1851, with his financial prospects improved, Samuel Ellis, 46, a boot and shoemaker, resided in Queen Street, Marylebone, London, with wife Susan, 48, and son William, 18, a boot closer.

Chapter 4

Thomas Gracie
Corporal 19024,
16th Battalion Royal Scots

Thomas Gracie (1889 – 1915)

Thomas Gracie was born on 12 June 1889 at 40 Edmund Street, Dennistoun, Glasgow, to father Robert Gracie, a master flesher or butcher, and mother Harriet Bell. Upon leaving school, Tom studied book-keeping before finding work as a meat salesman. He was concurrently playing Junior League football for Shawfield, then Strathclyde, but in 1907, he was offered the chance to move into League football when approached by Airdrieonians. After short spells with Hamilton Academical and Arthurlie, he joined Greenock Morton in 1909.

In 1911, Gracie was selected as a reserve for Scotland's game against England at Goodison Park, although he did not play. However, the trip proved fruitful, as he was signed by Everton at the international's conclusion. A season later he switched to the 'red half' of Merseyside, signing for Liverpool in an exchange deal. He was unable to establish himself in the Liverpool first team, making only sporadic appearances in his two and a half seasons at Anfield. When the opportunity arose to return to Scotland in 1914, he jumped at it.

Gracie signed for Hearts and manager John McCartney paid £400 for him. Under McCartney, Hearts proved a rapidly emerging side and started the 1914–15 season with eight straight victories, including a 2–0 victory over reigning champions Celtic, with Gracie scoring, becoming early league leaders and title favourites. Gracie was also selected for the Scottish League XI in November 1914.

However, this winning streak coincided with the outbreak of the Great War and the beginnings of a public debate upon the morality of continuing professional football while young soldiers were dying on the front-line. A motion was placed before the Scottish Football Association to postpone the season, with one of its backers, Airdrieonians chairman Thomas Forsyth, declaring that '*playing football while our men are fighting is repugnant*'. The noted East London philanthropist Frederick Charrington was orchestrating a public campaign to have professional football in Britain suspended. The prime tactic of Charrington's campaign was to shame football players and officials into action through public and private denouncement, and as Tom Gracie was then the leading scorer in the side at the top of the First Division in Scotland, he was an obvious target for the anti-football crusade.

A letter published in the *Edinburgh Evening News* on 16 November 1914 from 'Soldier's Daughter' suggested the team take the nom-de-plume of '*The White Feathers of Midlothian*'. Given that three Hearts' men had already signed with the colours, the article rankled with the other players at the suggestion they were all cowards.

Gracie's response, alongside ten of his team-mates, was to enlist in Sir George McCrae's new volunteer battalion, joining en-masse on 25 November 1914. Military training was then added to the Hearts players' football training regime. Although this did not initially stop the side's sporting progress, exhaustion from their army exertions eventually led to a drop in form. Defeats to St Mirren and Morton allowed Celtic to usurp the Maroons and eventually claim the league title by four points. For Gracie, finishing as the league's joint top-scorer was scant consolation.

Gracie, however, faced a much more serious problem. In March 1915, he was diagnosed with leukaemia, a prognosis he had shared only with manager McCartney. Despite his illness and against medical advice, he decided to continue to play with Hearts and train with the 16th Battalion. He was still with the battalion when they were sent south to Studley Royal Camp, Ripon, in June for further training. On 1 July 1915, a violent thunderstorm struck the camp killing five soldiers of the 15th Royal Scots. Willie Turnbull, a 29-year-old asylum attendant from Morningside, the 16th's only casualty, was carried off to hospital with shock and awoke to find Tom Gracie in the next bed. Gracie had succumbed to fatigue and he was then committed to a hospital in Leeds for treatment, before being transferred back to Glasgow's Stobhill Hospital.

On 23 October 1915, Sir George McCrae, recently returned from training in France, watched the 16th Battalion football team defeat the Northumberland Fusiliers in the final of the Divisional Championship. Duncan Currie scored four of the side's six goals. After the match, McCrae visited the players to tell them that Tom Gracie had died of leukaemia in Glasgow. This was a shock to the players as Tom had only let manager McCartney know of his illness. Hearts' director Sir James Leishman had visited Tom at his family home in Dennistoun and he wrote to McCartney, "I could easily discern that he was a good son and a loyal comrade; I feel convinced that he would have proved a first-class fighting man."

Corporal 19024 Thomas Gracie, 26, of 314 Duke Street, Dennistoun, Glasgow, died on 23 October 1915 in Stobhill Hospital, Glasgow of leukaemia and was buried at CWGC section P.107, Craigton Cemetery, Cardonald, Glasgow. His death concluded a dark year for the Gracie family, having also lost Tom's brother John at Loos and brother-in-law Tommy Reid at Gallipoli during 1915's hostilities.

Private 12547 John Bell Gracie, 5th Battalion Cameron Highlanders, 31, died on 28 September 1915 and he is buried in Bethune Town Cemetery, Pas de Calais, France. Tommy Reid had been a professional soldier prior to the war. When he married Isabella Gracie in 1903 he was based in Edinburgh Castle as a bandsman in the 42nd Regiment, the Black Watch, as a trombone player. Tommy re-enlisted as Private 1191 in the 1/7th Cameronians (Scottish Rifles) and, age 42, he was killed in action on 29 June 1915 and is buried in Twelve Tree Copse Cemetery, Gallipoli, Turkey.

Tom Gracie's widowed mother, Harriet, wrote to John McCartney, thanking him for bringing her son to Gorgie. She stated, "*He had found his home with Hearts and never was so happy.*"

Tom's parents - Robert Gracie and Harriet Bell

Tom's father Robert Gracie was born on 31 August 1847 at Lochfauld, Cadder, Lanarkshire, to father Thomas Gracie, a coal miner, and mother Margaret Chapman. The birth is recorded in the OPRs for Cadder (Ref: 626/3/100) as follows:-

1847: Gracie: Robert second lawful child of Thomas Gracie, Miner, and Margaret Chapman was born at Lochfauld August 31st & baptized October 3rd 1847

By 1851, his father Thomas was dead and Robert, 3, resided at No.32 Village of Banton, Stirlingshire, with his mother Margaret Gracie, only 27, a widow, and sister Barbry, 7, a scholar.

Tom's mother Harriet Bell, aka Heriot, was born around 1854 in Inveresk and Musselburgh, Midlothian to father John Bell, a lath-splitter journeyman, and mother Isabella Weir. In 1861, Heriot, 6, resided at Sanderson's Close, High Street, Musselburgh, with father John Bell, 46, a lath-splitter, mother Isabella, 40, and her siblings. In 1871, Harriet, just 16, was working as a housemaid at Newbigging House Lunatic Asylum, Inveresk under the proprietorship of Abram Moffat, 71, and his superintendent wife Euphemia, 66. The first patient listed was Charles F McKechnie, 71, formerly an artist, but now a deaf and dumb lunatic. There were some private patients, but most were listed as paupers and an 1857 report on the Moffat's institution described it in terms that were positively Dickensian, with tether-posts, seclusion rooms, and outside privies.

Robert Gracie, 28, a flesher, of 187 Eglinton Street, Gorbals, Glasgow, married Harriet Bell, 21, of 78 Commercial Road, Gorbals, Glasgow, on 31 August 1875 at 28 Abbotsford Place, Gorbals, Glasgow. The wedding was conducted by Rev William Rowe, minister of Laurieston Church of Scotland; the best man was James Lachlan and the best maid was Bethia Dunswood. Robert and Harriet had four known children in the infamous Gorbals district, later to become synonymous with Glasgow's *No Mean City* image of poverty, deprivation, gangs and crime. Their children were; Isabella (b. ~1877), Margaret (b. ~1880), John (b. ~1884) and Thomas (b. 12 June 1889).

In 1881, Robert Gracie, 33, a flesher, resided at 297 Eglinton Street, Gorbals, Glasgow, with wife Harriet, 26, daughters Isabella, 4, and Margaret, 1. Also lodging there was Robert's brother-in-law Colin Bell, 17, an iron moulder. Son Thomas Gracie was born on 12 June 1889 at 40 Edmund Street, Dennistoun, Glasgow. In 1903, the family were living at 19 Meadowpark Street, Dennistoun, when daughter Isabella Gracie married Black Watch bandsman Tommy Reid. Robert Gracie, a cattle dealer, was deceased by 1915, however, Harriet was still alive to suffer the heartache of her two sons Thomas and John dying in WW1, along with her daughter Isabella's husband Tommy Reid.

Tom's paternal grandparents -
Thomas Gracie and Margaret Chapman

Tom's paternal grandfather Thomas Gracie (or Grace) was born around 1819 in Banton, Stirlingshire. Banton was a tiny hamlet, which later became a coal mining village in the 19th century, but it has held its place in Scottish military history. It is recorded in '*Bell & Bain Ltd: a brief history*' that the Covenanter army under General William Baillie formed near Banton for their engagement with the Royalist forces under the command of the Duke of Montrose at the Battle of Kilsyth on 15 August 1645.

Tom's grandmother Margaret Chapman was born around 1824 in Kilsyth, Stirlingshire. Thomas Gracie, in Banton, married Margaret Chapman, in Kilsyth, on 8 February 1844 in Kilsyth Parish Church. The marriage is recorded in the OPRs for Kilsyth (Ref: 483/8/4) as follows:-

1844: Gracie and Chapman: 3 February: Thomas Gracie Banton and Margaret Chapman residing in this Parish have given in there [sic] names in order to proclamation of banns: 3 Sabbaths: Married by the Rev Henry Douglas 8th February 1844

Thomas, a coal miner, and Margaret had two known children; Barbara, aka Barbry (b. ~1844, Kilsyth) and Robert (b. 31 August 1847, Cadder). Son Robert Gracie was born on 31 August 1847 at Lochfauld, Cadder, Lanarkshire. It appears that Thomas Gracie was dead before his son Robert was born. Thomas Grace, 28, a labourer, of High Street, Glasgow, died on 5 March 1847 of typhus fever. Thomas was buried in the common ground of St Mungo's cemetery on 6 March 1847 by undertaker D. Carmichael.

The typhus epidemic, caused by infected lice, broke out in the west of Ireland in 1846, at the outbreak of the Irish Potato Famine. It spread to Ulster and Belfast in the winter of 1846–47 and impoverished Irish immigrants brought it into Britain, Canada and the USA. Thousands of Irish paupers died of typhus aboard overcrowded 'fever ships' and in quarantine 'fever camps' in Quebec, Montreal, and Philadelphia during 1847–48.

In 1851, Margaret Gracie, only 27, a widow, resided at No.32 Village of Banton, Stirlingshire, with daughter Barbry, 7, a scholar, son Robert, 3, and two coal mining lodgers to supplement her meagre income; Duncan McFarlane, 17, and George Gibbs, 18. Living next door at No.31 Village of Banton was Margaret's brother John Chapman, 33, a saddle maker, sister-in-law Janet Provan, 33, and their children John, 9, Janet, 7, both scholars, James, 5, Margaret, 2, Andrew, 6 months, and John's brother-in-law Andrew Provan, 35, a coal miner. Margaret remarried a second husband surnamed Cameron and she was still alive in 1875.

Tom's maternal grandparents –
John Bell and Isabella Weir

Tom's maternal grandfather John Bell was born around 1815 in Glasgow, Lanarkshire, and his grandmother Isabella Weir was born around 1821 in Liberton, Midlothian to father Alexander Weir. John Bell, a blacksmith in Cramond, married first wife, Isabella Dewar, in South Leith, in December 1834. The marriage is recorded in the OPRs for South Leith (Ref:

1834: Bell: John Bell, Blacksmith in Cramond, and
Isabella Dewar residing in the Parish of South Leith
and daughter of the late Alexander Dewar,
husbandman in the Parish of Aberdour, after
proclamation of banns were married

John and Isabella had a known son in Inveresk and Musselburgh; John (b. ~1844). Isabella Dewar must have died before 1850 as John, a lath-splitter, married second wife Isabella Weir on 14 December 1850 in Inveresk and Musselburgh. The marriage is recorded in the OPRs for Inveresk and Musselburgh (Ref: 689/19/325) as follows:-

1850: Bell: John, lath-splitter, residing in this parish
and Isabella Weir, daughter of Alexander Weir, also
residing in this parish, gave up their names for
proclamation of banns on 14th December 1850:
Cautioner for the man James Wilson & for the woman
Alexander Weir

John and Isabella had four known children in Musselburgh; George (b. ~1851), Harriet, aka Heriot (b. ~1854), Elizabeth Porteous (b. 6 February 1857) and Colin (b. 9 February 1864). No birth record has been found for Harriet, although she may have been baptized in a secessionist church such as the Free Church of Scotland. Daughter Elizabeth Porteous Bell was born on 6 February 1857 at Market Street, Fisherrow, Musselburgh.

In 1861, John Bell, 46, a lath-splitter, resided at Sanderson's Close, High Street, Musselburgh, with wife Isabella, 40, children John, 17, a currier, George, 10, Heriot, 6, and Elizabeth, 4, all scholars. Son Colin Bell was born on 9 February 1864 at High Street, Musselburgh, at which time John was working as a labourer at an oil mill. John Bell was dead by 1875, although, Isabella was still alive by then.

Tom's great-grandfather – Alexander Weir

Tom's maternal great-grandfather Alexander Weir was born around 1795 possibly in Midlothian. Alexander had a known daughter Isabella (b. ~1821, Liberton) and he was recorded as still alive in 1850 in Inveresk and Musselburgh, where he stood as cautioner or witness at his daughter Isabella's wedding.

Chapter 5

James Hawthorn
Private 19038,
16th Battalion Royal Scots

James Hawthorn (1875 – 1916)

James Hawthorn (or Hawthorne) was born on 6 November 1875 at Calderbank, Old Monkland, Lanarkshire, to father George Hawthorn, a brick moulder, and mother Lillias Gilchrist. In 1881, James, 5, a scholar, resided at South Side of the street, Kirknewton, East Calder, Midlothian, with his father George Hawthorn, 25, a brick maker, mother Lillie, 24, and his siblings. The family later moved to Prestonpans, East Lothian and, after leaving school, Jimmy became a kiln burner at the Prestongrange Brickworks.

James Hawthorn, 22, a kiln burner, of 14 Cuthill, Prestonpans, married Agnes Ritchie, 22, of 1 Hawthorn Terrace, Cockenzie on Hogmanay, 31 December 1897. The wedding was conducted by Rev George S Smith, minister of Prestonpans Church of Scotland; the best man was John Doig and the best maid was Fanny Stevenson. In January 1898, Hawthorn was signed as a full-back for Hearts and he made a few appearances between January and March 1899, playing alongside Hearts greats Charlie Thomson and Bobby Walker.

On Saturday 5 December 1915, Hearts were playing Hibernian in the first derby match of the season. The Gorgie club granted free admission to Tynecastle to any man who had enrolled in the new Service Battalions and 800 men took up the invitation. At two o'clock, preceded by the pipe band of the 9th Royal Scots, Sir George McCrae led the newly enlisted men into Tynecastle to rapturous applause. Wattie, Gracie, and Low scored in a fine 3–1 victory over Hibs.

That same evening Jimmy Hawthorn attended a meeting in Portobello Town Hall. He was there with his companions and they had been celebrating Hearts win with a few drinks. Hawthorn, by then 40, was a former Hearts player, a back-line partner of the great Charlie Thomson, and one of Bobby Walker's drinking pals. At the time, he was working as a contractor at Prestongrange Brickworks. Moved to tears at the meeting, Hawthorn and his pals set off to Edinburgh, vowing to enlist and remain pals for life. When he awoke from his alcoholic haze the next morning, Hawthorn discovered he was the only one of the group who had actually enlisted.

On 1 July 1916, Jimmy was amongst Captain Lionel Cole's C Company who had remained largely intact by mid-morning on that dreadful first day of the Battle of the Somme. Around late morning, Cole led another charge towards La Boisselle and Hawthorn went up alongside his Hearts pals. They emerged from the sunken road straight into a nest of German machine-guns. Ernie Ellis and Jimmy Hawthorn both fell in front of the wire. Further up the road, Duncan Currie was hit in the right shoulder and Harry Wattie also fell in a hail of bullets.

Hawthorn's body was never recovered. Private 19038 James Hawthorn is commemorated on the Thiepval Memorial, on the same Pier and Faces 6D and 7D as his Hearts pals Ernie Ellis, Jimmy Boyd, and Duncan Currie. He is also commemorated on the CWGC website. Private 19038 James Hawthorn was posthumously awarded the Victory and British War medals.

Jimmy's parents -
George Hawthorn and Lillias Gilchrist

Jimmy's father George Hawthorn was born around 1856 in the United States of America to Irish parents, father James Hawthorn, a joiner, and mother Margaret Christie. His mother Lillias Gilchrist, aka Lillie, was born on 8 June 1856 at Calderbank, Old Monkland, Lanarkshire, to father Thomas Gilchrist, an iron puddler, and mother Jane Smith.

In 1871, George Hawthorn, 15, a labourer, resided at 14 Post Office Row, Calderbank, with his mother Margaret, 32, step-father James Purvis, 27, an iron works labourer, and his siblings. George Hawthorn, 19, a brick moulder, of New Square Row, Calderbank, married Lillias Gilchrist, 18, a domestic servant, of Post Office Row, Calderbank, on 11 September 1874. The wedding was conducted by Rev John Smith, minister of Calderbank Church of Scotland; the best man was Alexander Gilchrist, Lillie's brother, and the best maid was Annie Reside.

George and Lillie had three known children; James (b. 6 November 1875, Calderbank), Margaret (b. ~1878, Bothwell) and Jane (b. ~1880, Portobello). In 1881, George Hawthorn, 25, a brick maker, resided on the South Side of the street, Kirknewton, East Calder, Midlothian, with wife Lillie, 24, children James, 5, a scholar, Margaret, 3, and Jane, 1. In 1891, George, a brick maker, and Lillias were still living in Prestonpans.

Jimmy's paternal grandparents - James Hawthorn and Margaret Christie

Jimmy's paternal grandfather James Hawthorn was born around 1825 in County Down, Ireland. His paternal grandmother Margaret Christie was born around 1828 in County Down to father John Christie, a farmer, and mother Jane Drysdale. After James, a joiner to trade, and Margaret married, they joined the post-Irish Potato Famine exodus and emigrated to the United States of America where they had a known son George (b. ~1856), although they returned to Ireland, where they had a known daughter Mary (b. ~1863).

James was dead by 1866 and Margaret remarried a second husband, Irish-born James Purvis on 26 February 1866 in Calderbank. Margaret and James Purvis had two sons in Calderbank; James (b. ~1868) and John (b. 24 April 1869). In 1871, Margaret, 32, resided at 14 Post Office Row, Calderbank, with husband James Purvis, 27, an iron works labourer, children George Hawthorn, 15, a labourer, Mary Hawthorn, 8, a scholar, James Purvis, 3, and John Purvis, 1. In 1901, Margaret, 70, resided at 13 Springfield Road, Bishopbriggs, Cadder, with husband James Purvis, 55, an engine keeper. Margaret Purvis previously Hawthorn nee Christie, 74, died on 3 June 1902 at home in Bishopbriggs of a cerebral haemorrhage and paralysis as certified by Dr James B Miller MB ChB.

Jimmy's maternal grandparents –
Thomas Gilchrist and Jane Smith

Jimmy's maternal grandfather Thomas Gilchrist and his grandmother Jane Smith were both born around 1825 probably in Lanarkshire. Thomas Gilchrist, an iron shingler, at the Calderbank Ironworks, married Jane Smith on 12 December 1852 in Calderbank, Old Monkland. The marriage is recorded in the OPRs for Coatbridge or Old Monkland (Ref: 652/3/472) as follows:-

1852: December: 12: Thomas Gilchrist, shingler, and Jane Smith both at Calderbank Works in this parish

Daughter Lillias Gilchrist, aka Lillie, was born on 8 June 1856 at Calderbank, Old Monkland, Lanarkshire, to father Thomas Gilchrist, an iron puddler, and mother Jane Smith. Thomas and Jane were still alive in 1874 and living at Post Office Row, Calderbank. The Calderbank Ironworks was founded in 1835 and by 1887 it had grown to 6 blast furnaces and 60 puddling furnaces, with a reversing mill producing malleable iron boiler and ships' plates, however, it went into decline in the 1890s.

Jimmy's paternal great-grandparents –
John Christie and Jane Drysdale

Jimmy's paternal great-grandfather John Christie and great-grandmother Jane Drysdale were born around 1800 in County Down, Ireland. John and Jane had a known daughter Margaret (b. ~1828) in County Down. John Christie, a farmer, and wife Jane were both dead before 1902.

Chapter 6

Henry Wattie
Private 19112,
16th Battalion Royal Scots

Henry Wattie (1891 – 1916)

Harry Benzie Wattie, aka Henry, was born on 3 June 1891 at 8 Livingstone Place, Newington, Edinburgh, to father William Wattie, a coachman, and mother Jessie Benzie. A boyhood Hearts fan, Harry was educated at Boroughmuir High School and played for several Junior sides, including Tranent, only formed in 1911. John McCartney signed him from Tranent in 1913. In his first-team debut at Tynecastle against Rangers, Wattie ran the game and scored two winning goals. Recently retired Hearts legend Bobby Walker, watching the game, reported, *"I think the boss has found a good 'un".* Wattie's sister Alice became engaged to his teammate and best friend Pat Crossan.

Wattie was part of the Hearts contingent of 11 players who enlisted in McCrae's Battalion on 25 November 1914. At a packed meeting in the Usher Hall on Friday 27 November, the recruiting for McCrae's 16th Royal Scots began in earnest. John McCartney, who was present, would later write, *"There was a rousing ovation, the sheer power, and volume of which, nearly knocked me off my feet. I looked along at Currie on my right. He was exactly the colour of milk. Crossan, too. And poor old Harry Wattie looked quite ill."*

On 5 March 1915, the French army conducted an offensive at the Battle of Hartmannwillerskopf on the French-German border. That same day, while still playing for Hearts and doing his military training, Harry Wattie, of 12 Marchmont Road, Morningside, Edinburgh, had the sad duty of registering the death of his father William.

On 5 May 1916, the 16th Battalion detrained at Longeau, near the Somme region, and marched towards Raineville, with a nine-hour march to Houlle. Piper Willie Duguid, nicknamed Duggie, blasted out 'Bonnie Dundee' in the heat and the battalion sang Private George Blaney's verse composed at Ripon.

Just a twelve-month ago Private Wattie was said,
To be sure of a national cap for his head,
Now he wears the Glengarry, right proud of the day,
That he marched to the standard of Geordie McCrae!

On 7 May, almost two months before the dreaded battle, Wattie wrote home from his tent outside the village of Houlle.

"We travelled all night in the train, forty to a cattle-truck, and then had a ten-mile march, so we were pretty fed up when we landed. I enjoyed the journey, though, as we came through some lovely country...I believe it will be even warmer here. I don't know how long it will be before we go back to the trenches, but it won't be so bad if this weather holds good...Every one of us is as brown as a berry and we are all in the best of health."

On the eve of battle on 30 June, many of the men of the 16th scribbled down their 'Soldier's Short Form of Will' in their Pay Book. Wattie left everything to his recently widowed mother and advised her that Hearts might be prepared to help her out if the worst happened. Before the whistles blew at 7.30am on 1 July, the 16th sat pensively on the fire-step of the front-line trench. Private Murdie McKay, a 24-year-old lithographer from Logan Street, was with Duncan Currie. McKay said that most of the Hearts men were together at the last. Crossan was quiet; he and Wattie had sat with Jimmy Hazeldean. Alfie Briggs and Teddy McGuire were writing home. Ernie Ellis was waiting with Sam Brindley. Annan Ness and Jimmy Boyd were up at Company HQ. Sir George McCrae came down the communication trench to see the lads off but found the trenches beyond Monymusk Street trench far too crowded to continue.

By late morning, Captain Lionel Cole's C Company had remained fairly intact, reaching the sunken road leading into La Boisselle. Cole ordered another try for the village, but as they emerged they came under sustained German machine-gun fire. Ellis, Hawthorn, and Hazeldean were all caught in the hail of bullets. Annan Ness saw Duncan Currie and Harry Wattie both fall. Wattie's body was never recovered.

Private 19112 Henry Wattie is commemorated on the Thiepval Memorial, on the same Pier and Faces 6D and 7D as his Hearts pals Ernie Ellis, Jimmy Boyd, Duncan Currie, and Jimmy Hawthorn. He is also commemorated on the CWGC website. He was posthumously awarded the Victory and

British War medals. Wattie never lived to achieve the Scotland international cap he so rightly deserved.

Harry's parents - William Wattie and Jessie Benzie

Harry's father William Wattie was born on 22 October 1832 in Holburn Street, Old Machar, Aberdeenshire, to father William Wattie, a labourer, and mother Margaret Milne. The birth is recorded in the OPRs for Old Machar (Ref: 168/B/13/151) as follows:-

1832: William Wattie, Labourer, Holborn St. & his Spouse Margaret Milne, had a son born on the 22nd day of October 1832 named William, baptized by the Revd Dr Kidd in presence of his Congregation

Harry's mother Janet Benzie, aka Jessie, was born on 7 July 1848 at Craigmancey, Inverkeithny, Banffshire, to father James Benzie, a farmer, and mother Janet Morrison. The birth is recorded in the OPRs for Inverkeithny (Ref: 158/2/44) as follows:-

1848: (Born July 7th) July 22nd: Benzies: Janet lawful child of James Benzies in Craigmancey & Janet Morrison his spouse and baptized before witnesses Alexander Benzies & Peter Wilson

William Wattie, 35, a farmer, of Balveen Cottage, Inverkeithny, married Jessie Benzie, 21, a farmer's daughter, of Mains of Craigmancey, Inverkeithny, on 30 December 1869 at the Benzie farm. The wedding was conducted by Rev John Lauder, minister of Inverkeithny Parish Church of

Scotland; the best man was John Wattie, William's brother, and the best maid was Ann Findlay. William and Jessie had 11 known children; in Inverkeithny, Annie (b. ~1869), Margaret, aka Maggie (b. ~1871), in Leith, James (b. ~1876), William (b. ~1878), Agnes (b. ~1879), Robert (b. ~1883), John (b. ~1885), Mary (b. ~1888), in Edinburgh, Louisa (b. ~1889), Harry Benzie (b. 3 June 1891) and Alice (b. >1892).

In 1881, William Wattie, stated as 36, although nearer 49, a cabman, resided at 16 Balfour Street, Leith, with wife Jessie, 32, children Annie, 12, Margaret, 10, James, 5, all scholars, William, 3, and Agnes, 2. Also boarding at William's home was David Reid, 48, a groom, and Donald McLean, 27, a warehouseman. In 1891, William Wattie, 46, although nearer 59, a coachman, resided at 8 Livingstone Place, Edinburgh, with wife Jessie, 42, children Maggie, 20, a dressmaker, James, 15, a telegraph messenger, William, 13, a baker, Agnes, 12, Robert, 8, John, 6, all scholars, Mary, 3, and Louisa, 2.

Jessie was heavily pregnant at that time and son Harry Benzie Wattie, aka Henry, was born on 3 June 1891 at 8 Livingstone Place, Newington, Edinburgh. By the outbreak of WW1 the family were living at 12 Marchmont Road, Morningside, Edinburgh, close to Warrender Park.

William Wattie, stated as 70, a coachman domestic, died on 3 March 1915 at 12 Marchmont Road, Morningside, Edinburgh of bronchitis and emphysema, myocarditis and influenza as certified by Dr W S McLaren MB. The death was registered by his son Henry Wattie on 5 March 1915 at the Edinburgh Registry Office. Jessie was left a widow and she would also lose her son Harry the following July at the

Somme. Jessie Wattie nee Benzie, 78, died in 1927 in Edinburgh.

Harry's paternal grandparents -
William Wattie and Margaret Jane Milne

Harry's paternal grandfather William Wattie and his grandmother Margaret Jane Milne were born around 1805 in Aberdeenshire. William Wattie married Margaret Milne on 29 November 1831 in Rhynie and Essie, Aberdeenshire. The marriage is recorded in the OPRs for Rhynie and Essie (Ref: 237/A/2/203) as follows:-

1831: Wattie & Milne: William Wattie and Margaret Milne both in this Parish having been proclaimed were married November 29th 1831, before these Witnesses Robert Milne at New Meldrum and William Mill farmer at New Town of Alford

William and Margaret had two known sons; William and John. Son William Wattie was born on 22 October 1832 in Holburn Street, Old Machar, Aberdeenshire, to father William Wattie, a labourer, and mother Margaret Milne. William, a farmer, was dead by 1869, although, his wife Margaret was still alive by then, although she was certainly dead by 1915.

Harry's maternal grandparents –
James Benzie and Janet Morrison

Harry's maternal grandfather James Benzie (or Benzies) was born in 1815 in Inverkeithny, Banffshire and his grandmother

Janet Morrison, aka Jessie, was born around 1823 in Grange, Banffshire. James Benzie and Janet Morrison were married on 11 December 1845 in Inverkeithny. The marriage is recorded in the OPRs for Inverkeithny (Ref: 158/2/89) as follows:-

1845: November 29th: James Benzies and Janet or Jessy Morrison both in this parish contracted in order to marriage, consigned pledged and were after due proclamations married December 11th

James, a farmer, and Janet had 11 known children; including Alexander, William, Robert, Harry Anderson, Janet and Ann. Daughter Janet Benzie, aka Jessie, was born on 7 July 1848 at Craigmancey, Inverkeithny, Banffshire. Daughter Ann was born on 8 April 1851 at Craigmancey. James, a farmer, and Janet were still alive in 1869 living at Mains of Craigmancey. Janet Benzie nee Morrison, 82, died in 1905.

Chapter 7

Alfred Briggs
Corporal 18980,
16th Battalion Royal Scots

Alfred Briggs (1888 – 1950)

Alfred Ernest Briggs was born on 4 February 1888 at 9 Northburn Street, Milton, Glasgow, to father Walter Alfred Ernest Briggs, a drapery warehouseman, aka Alfred, and mother Jane Fullarton Phillips, aka Jessie. This was the old district of Milton just north of the city centre, which included Cowcaddens and Port Dundas, and much of it was demolished in the 1960s and 70s to make way for the M8 motorway. In 1891, Alfred, 3, resided at 35 Crawford Street, Partick, Glasgow, with his father Alfred Briggs, 30, a coachman, mother Jessie, 26, and sisters Agnes, 4, and Emma, 1.

In 1901, Alfred, 13, a scholar, resided at 18 Cross Street, Partick, with his father Alfred Briggs, 40, a coachman domestic, mother Jessie, 36, and his siblings. Before becoming a professional footballer, Briggs worked as a sewing machine builder for the world-renowned Singer Sewing Machine Corporation in Clydebank. In 1911, Alfred, 22, a machine builder, resided at Broomhill Lane off Broomhill Road, Partick, with his father Alfred Briggs, 50, a coachman in domestic service, mother Jessie, 46, and his other siblings.

While working at the Singer Works, Briggs began his football career at Clydebank Juniors at the original Kilbowie Park. After being capped by the Scotland Junior team in 1912, he was signed by Hearts manager John McCartney as a professional wing-half. He was in the Hearts team that won the Rosebery Charity Cup in 1912–13. Briggs made 70 appearances for the club between 1912 and 1917, but he was forced to retire due to wounds sustained during WW1.

After the outbreak of the war in August 1914, Briggs enlisted, on that same day 25 November 1914, as ten of his teammates, as a Corporal in McCrae's Battalion. On 27 January 1916, the Kaiser's birthday, Sir George McCrae received orders for the 16th to go up to the front-line for their first garrison action. They had been billeted in dreadful conditions at Fort Rompu, south of Armentieres. At 8pm it was 'pitch black and quiet' when the battalion arrived at Bois Grenier, marching along a long communication trench, called Shaftesbury Avenue, and up to the firing line for a four-day garrison of the sector.

The Kaiser's birthday celebrations concluded with the heaviest German bombardment ever seen in the sector. For Alfie Briggs, the worst part was the fierce rattle of machine-guns.

It comes right along the line, every bullet just skipping the parapet, Briggs wrote to McCartney.

On 12 March, Coles' C Company was back in the line, when the Germans opened up a hurricane bombardment. Six C Company privates were wounded, including Raith Rovers winger Private 19109 Jimmy Todd, a 20-year-old railway clerk, son of Robert and Jessie Todd of 41 Easter Road,

Edinburgh. Todd was hit by a large shell fragment in the chest and died before the bombardment ended. Briggs attended Todd's funeral at Erquinghem-Lys Churchyard Extension and he wrote to McCartney, "Jimmy was in everything, a constant source of solace to us all with his good humour and cheerfulness. He is a sore loss."

On the morning of 1 July, Briggs was spotted sitting on the fire-step, writing a letter home. At 8am, Sir George McCrae received a message that the battalion had attacked. The leading companies had fought their way through the barbed wire, flanked Heligoland, and crossed Kipper Trench, only to get bunched up on the second German line. A German machine-gun was causing carnage.

Briggs was badly wounded near La Boisselle on that first day of the Battle of the Somme, being *hit by four machine-gun bullets; one in his leg, another in his left foot and through his arm, another in his right ankle, coming out above the knee and another winging his forehead, knocking him out.* He sought refuge in a shell hole just behind the alley, where German hand grenade bombers actually crawled over him during abortive counter attacks that night. He was found barely alive the next day and returned to an advanced dressing station near Bécourt, where he was fully expected to die. However, an orderly noticed he was still breathing and he made a recovery before being returned to Epsom Hospital in Surrey to recuperate.

Private 18980 Alfred Briggs was awarded the Victory and British War medals. He also received a Silver War Badge for being wounded in action and he was honourably discharged. Briggs recovered from his wounds but never played professional football again. He later returned to work after the war as a boilermaker. He suffered from periods of black depression, especially around 1 July and Remembrance Days, which nowadays would have been diagnosed as post-traumatic stress disorder.

He later returned to play in Peter Nellies' testimonial match in April 1921 and he had a spell working as a talent scout for Partick Thistle. Between 1920–21 and 1925–26, Alfred Briggs resided at 94 Hozier Street, Partick, Glasgow, with an annual rent of £20 5s. On 17 March 1941, just three days after the Clydebank Blitz, which caused significant damage to his old Singer Works, Alfie Briggs, of 22 Esslemont Avenue, Scotstoun, Glasgow, registered the death of his father Walter A E Briggs, 77, at the Glasgow Registry Office. At the time of his death in 1950, Briggs, only 61, still had two German bullets lodged in his spine.

Alfie's parents – Walter Alfred Ernest Briggs and Jane Fullarton Phillips

Alfie's father Walter Alfred Ernest Briggs, aka Alfred, was born around November 1860 in St Mary's, Birkenhead, Cheshire, to father Jonathan Briggs, a railway conductor, and mother Emma Ann Dale. Walter was christened on 7 November 1860 at St Mary's Church, Birkenhead in Cheshire. In 1861, baby Walter A E, resided at Tranmere Park, Birkenhead, Cheshire, with his mother Emma A Briggs, 25, brothers Arthur H J, 2, Albert R J, 1, and. his widowed great-grandmother Elizabeth Broadhurst, 77.

Alfie's mother Jane Fullarton Phillips, aka Jessie, was born on 24 March 1865 at 9 Cedar Place, Milton, Glasgow to father John Phillips, an iron moulder, and mother Agnes Clark.

By 1869, Alfred's father Jonathan was dead and his mother remarried Robert Murdoch in 1870 in Liverpool, the family then moving to Blythswood, Glasgow in the following year. In 1881, Alfred Briggs, 20, a draper's assistant, resided at 196 Sauchiehall Street, Blythswood, Glasgow, with his mother Emma A Murdoch, 46, step-father Robert, 48, a commission agent, and his siblings. The terraced tenement on Sauchiehall Street was the establishment of Muirhead & Coy, silk stockings and drapery warehousemen, and it is likely Alfred worked there as a drapery assistant.

Walter A E Briggs, 24, a drapery warehouseman, residing at 15 Windsor Street, Milton, Glasgow, married Jane F Phillips, 20, residing at 4 Grove Street, Milton, Glasgow, on Hogmanay, 31 December 1885 at Jane's home. The wedding was conducted by Rev I McDougall, minister of the United Presbyterian Church; the best man was James Bruce Walker Jr and the best maid was Helen Phillips, Jane's sister.

Alfred and Jessie had eight known children, with one child dying in childhood; in Glasgow, Agnes (b. ~1887), Alfred (b. 4 February 1888), Emma (b. ~1890), John (b. ~1892), Helen, aka Nellie (b. ~1898), Margaret, aka Maggie (b. ~1900), Jeanie (b. ~1903), and in Stirling, Jessie Phillips (b. 18 August 1893). Son Alfred Ernest Briggs was born on 4 February 1888 at 9 Northburn Street, Milton, Glasgow.

In 1891, Alfred Briggs, 30, a coachman, resided at 35 Crawford Street, Partick, Glasgow, with wife Jessie, 26, children Agnes, 4, Alfred, 3, and Emma, 1. Daughter Jessie Phillips Briggs was born on 18 August 1893 at The Parsonage, Dunmore Park, Airth, although, the family still lived at 35 Crawford Street. The Parsonage was part of the Murray family estate of Dunmore Park, the Earl of Dunmore having bought the estate of Elphinstone Pans and redeveloped it into a model village for his estate workers. Alfred, who registered Jessie's birth on 7 September 1893 at the Airth Registry Office, may have been working temporarily as a coachman at Dunmore Park. The Parsonage is now an elite private home and exclusive wedding venue.

In 1901, Alfred Briggs, 40, a coachman domestic, resided at 18 Cross Street, Partick, with wife Jessie, 36, children Agnes, 14, a lithographic worker, Alfred, 13, Emma, 11, John, 9, Jessie, 7, all four scholars, Nellie, 3, and Maggie, 1. In 1905–06, Alfred resided at 21 Cross Street, Partick with an annual rent of £12.

In 1911, Alfred Briggs, 50, a coachman in domestic service, resided at Broomhill Lane off Broomhill Road, Partick, with wife Jessie, 46, children Alfred, 22, a sewing machine builder, Emma, 21, a brusher at an enamel works doing street numbers and names, John, 19, a coachbuilder, Jessie, 17, a fish shop clerkess, Nellie, 13, Maggie, 11, and Jeanie, 8, all three at school. It is unclear who Alfred was coachman for in the upmarket district of Broomhill, however, the closest villa to the lane was Mrs Margaret Ferguson, 77, a woman of private means, residing in Larkfield House, Broomhill Road, Partick. Broomhill is now designated as an outstanding architectural conservation area.

In 1915–16, during WW1, Alfred, a coachman, resided at 15 India Street, Partick with an annual rent of £13 5s and he was still living there in 1920–21. In 1925–26, Alfred, a coachman, resided at 75 Chancellor Street, Partick with an annual rent of £18 15s. Alfred's wife Jessie Fullarton Briggs nee Phillips, 64, died in 1929 in Partick, Glasgow.

Two days after the devastating Clydebank Blitz on 13 and 14 March 1941, during WW2, which had targeted John Brown's Shipyards and the Singer Works, where son Alfie once worked, Walter Alfred Ernest Briggs, 80, a retired and widowed coachman, of 69 Medwyn Street, Whiteinch, Glasgow, died on 16 March 1941 in the Southern General Hospital, Govan, of senility and hypostatic pneumonia as certified by Dr G M Clark MB ChB. The death was registered by his son Alfred Briggs on 17 March 1941 at the Glasgow Registry Office.

Alfie's paternal grandparents –
Jonathan Briggs and Emma Ann Dale

Alfie's paternal grandfather Jonathan Briggs, aka John, was born around 1834 in Bosley, Cheshire and his grandmother Emma Ann Dale was born around 1836 in nearby Henbury, Cheshire to father James Dale, a farmer, and mother Elizabeth Morris Broadhurst. Jonathan Briggs married Emma Ann Dale in the 4th Quarter of 1857 in Liverpool, Lancashire as registered in Vol. 8b and Page 173 at the Liverpool Registry Office. Jonathan and Emma had three known sons in St

Mary's parish, Birkenhead; Arthur Henry James (b. 18 Aug 1858), Herbert Randolph John (b. 21 Sep 1859) and Walter Alfred Ernest (b. 7 November 1860).

Son Walter Alfred Ernest Briggs, aka Alfred, was born around November 1860 in Birkenhead, Cheshire, to father Jonathan Briggs, a railway conductor, and mother Emma Ann Dale. He was christened on 7 November 1860 at St Mary's Church, Birkenhead in Cheshire. In 1861, John Briggs, 27, a labourer, was working away from home, and was lodging at Mill Lane, Failsworth, Manchester. His wife Emma A Briggs, 25, resided at Tranmere Park, Birkenhead, Cheshire, with sons Arthur H J, 2, Albert R J, 1, and baby Walter A E. Also residing at Emma's home was her grandmother Elizabeth Broadhurst, 77, a widow, and Anne Whitby, 21, a female servant.

Jonathan or John Briggs, recorded as a civil engineer, was dead by 1869 and his wife Emma Ann Briggs remarried second husband Robert Murdoch, a clothier, on 1 January 1870 in Edge Hill, Liverpool. Robert Murdoch was born around 1833 in Torrance, Stirlingshire. Robert and Emma moved to Glasgow around 1871.

Robert and Emma Ann had two known sons born in Blythswood, Glasgow; Claude Alexander Harold Briggs Murdoch (b. 8 November 1871) and Robert Albert Napier Murdoch (b. 17 May 1873). In 1881, Emma A Murdoch, 46, resided at 196 Sauchiehall Street, Blythswood, Glasgow, with husband Robert, 48, a commission agent, children Arthur Briggs, 22, Herbert Briggs, 21, both bank clerks, Alfred Briggs, 20, a draper's assistant, Claude Murdoch, 9, and Albert Murdoch, 7. Emma Ann Murdoch, previously Briggs nee Dale, only 52, died on 11 May 1886 at 15 Windsor Street, Kelvin, Glasgow of cancer of the stomach and debility as certified by Dr John A Lothian MD. The death was registered by her son Herbert R J Briggs on 12 May 1886 at the Glasgow Registry Office.

Alfie's maternal grandparents – John McDonald Phillips and Agnes Clark

Alfie's maternal grandfather John McDonald Phillips was born around 1836 in Stenhousemuir, Larbert, Stirlingshire to father Thomas Phillips, an iron moulder, and mother Agnes McDonald. In 1841, John, 5, resided at Carronshore, Larbert, with his father Thomas Phillips, 35, an iron moulder, mother Agnes, 40, and his other siblings. Another famous footballing lineage associated with Carronshore is detailed in *Pride of the Jocks* by Derek Niven. Eddie Turnbull, one of Hibernian's Famous Five, and later manager of Aberdeen and Hibs, was born on 12 April 1923 at Carronshore.

After leaving school, John started as an apprentice iron moulder at the renowned Carron Iron Works. Alfie's grandmother Agnes Clark was born around 1840 in Glasgow, Lanarkshire to father John Clark, a malt man, and mother Janet Fullarton.

John Phillips, 23, an iron moulder, married first wife Jane Vassie Denholm, 19, a weaver, both of 124½ Garscube Road, Milton, Glasgow on Hogmanay, 31 December 1858 at 202 Renfrew Street, Glasgow. The wedding was conducted by Rev William Cochrane, minister of the Church of Scotland; the best man was David Crawford and the best maid was

Elizabeth Scott. Jane was the daughter of John Denholm, a deceased spirit dealer, and mother Mary Winning.

Within a few months following the marriage, Jane fell pregnant, but things went tragically wrong during childbirth. Jane Vassie Phillips nee Denholm, only 19, died on 20 December 1859 at 124½ Garscube Road, Milton, Glasgow of puerperal peritonitis, for four days, as certified by Dr George McGregor MD, 'who saw the deceased 20th December'. Puerperal peritonitis is a bacterial infection of the female reproductive organs following childbirth or miscarriage. The death was registered by widower John McD Phillips on 21 December 1859 at the Glasgow Registry Office. Jane was buried in Sighthill Cemetery, Springburn, Glasgow, with Wylie & Lochhead, the long-established Glasgow undertakers, officiating at her burial.

In 1861, John Phillips, 25, a widowed iron moulder, resided at 13 Cameron Street, Maryhill, Glasgow, with his mother-in-law Mary Denholm, 49, a washerwoman. Also, living up the same tenement close at 13 Cameron Street, were John's two brothers; unmarried Thomas, 18, an iron moulder, and married William, 34, also an iron moulder, and his family.

John Phillips, 28, an iron moulder, married second wife Agnes Clark, 24, a steam loom weaver, both of 115 Garscube Road, Milton, Glasgow on 24 June 1864. The wedding was conducted by Rev John Barclay, minister of the United Presbyterian Church; the best man was James Clark, Agnes's brother, and the best maid was Emma Clough.

Daughter Jane Fullarton Phillips, aka Jessie, was born on 24 March 1865 at 9 Cedar Place, Milton, Glasgow to father

John Phillips, an iron moulder, and mother Agnes Clark. John, an iron moulder journeyman, and Agnes were both still alive in Glasgow in 1885.

Alfie's paternal great-grandparents – James Dale and Elizabeth Morris Broadhurst

Alfie's paternal great-grandfather James Dale and his great-grandmother Elizabeth Morris Broadhurst were both born around 1810 possibly in Henbury, Cheshire. James Dale, a farmer, married Elizabeth Morris Broadhurst and they had a known daughter Emma Ann Dale born around 1836 in Henbury, Cheshire. James Dale, a farmer, was still alive in 1886, although, his wife Elizabeth was dead by then.

Alfie's maternal great-grandparents – Thomas Phillips and Agnes McDonald

Alfie's maternal great-grandfather Thomas Phillips was born around 1805 and his great-grandmother Agnes McDonald was born around 1801 in Stirlingshire. Thomas Phillips worked as an iron moulder at the renowned Carron Iron Works, famous for its carronade cannons used at the Battle of Trafalgar in 1805 and by the Royal Navy up to 1850.

In 1820, there was a short-lived minor rebellion against the Westminster Government called the Radical Rising, seeking Scottish independence. The poorly-armed radicals, led from Glasgow by Andrew Hardie and joined at Condorrat by ex-soldier John Baird, marched towards the

Carron Iron Works. The workers at Carron were currently on strike. Hardie and Baird believed that about 2,000 Carron workers would join the rebellion, providing carronades and munitions. However, Government spies were well aware of the plan and the rebel force was tricked into hiding at Bonnymuir, where a cavalry charge by a troop of Hussars, swiftly forced the rebels to surrender.

It is not known whether Thomas had started work at Carron during the abortive strike, but he would have certainly known all about it. Thomas Phillips, an iron moulder, married Agnes McDonald and they had five known children in Larbert; William (b. ~1826), Margaret (b. ~1828), Helen (b. ~1830), John McDonald (b. ~1836) and Thomas (b. ~1843).

Son John McDonald Phillips was born around 1836 in Stenhousemuir, Larbert, Stirlingshire. In 1841, Thomas Phillips, 35, an iron moulder, resided at Carronshore, Larbert, with wife Agnes, 40, children William, 15, an apprentice moulder, Margaret, 13, Helen, 11, and John, 5. Thomas and Agnes were both dead by 1859.

Alfie's maternal great-grandparents – John Clark and Janet Fullarton

Alfie's other maternal great-grandfather John Clark and great-grandmother Janet Fullarton were both born around 1815 possibly in Glasgow, Lanarkshire. John Clark, a malt man in a whisky distillery, married Janet Fullarton and they had a daughter Agnes (b. ~1840) and a son James in Glasgow. John, a malt man, was dead by 1864, although, his wife Janet was still alive by then.

Alfie's paternal great-great-grandmother – Elizabeth Broadhurst

Alfie's paternal great-great-grandmother Elizabeth Broadhurst (her married name) was born around 1784 in Teddington, Cheshire. She had a known daughter Elizabeth Morris Broadhurst born about 1810 possibly in Henbury, Cheshire. In 1861, Elizabeth, 77, a widow, was recorded as 'grandmother to the head of household' living at Tranmere Park, Birkenhead, with her granddaughter Emma A Briggs, 25, and her three grandsons.

Chapter 8

Patrick Crossan
Private 18998,
16th Battalion Royal Scots

Patrick Crossan (1891 – 1933)

Patrick James Crossan was born on 21 May 1891 at 7 Baker Street, Addiewell, West Calder, to father Edward Crossan, a fireman in a shale mine, and mother Bridget Nicholas. In 1901, Patrick, 9, a scholar, resided at 3 Simpson Street, Addiewell, West Calder, with his father Edward Crossan, 33, a shale oil works labourer, mother Bridget, 35, and his siblings. Crossan was a professional footballer who played in defence for Hearts. He was known as Paddy in the footballing press, but he preferred to be called Pat in the dressing room.

Crossan joined Hearts from Arniston Rangers on 8 November 1911 alongside his pal Willie Wilson. At the time, he lodged at Wilson's family home, close to the Tynecastle ground. He was a powerful and extremely fast runner, supplementing his income occasionally by racing in athletics professionally under pseudonyms. Crossan was renowned as a handsome man and his teammate Harry Wattie joked, "*Pat can maybe pass the ball, but he couldn't pass a mirror if he tried!*" Crossan became engaged to Harry's sister Alice Wattie.

After the outbreak of the war in August 1914, Crossan enlisted on 26 November 1914 in McCrae's Battalion of the Royal Scots. The following Thursday he joined McCrae for recruitment meetings at Younger's Brewery in Abbeyhill and Miller's Foundry in London Road. One man stepped forward but he was obviously married. *"Have you got bairns?"* enquired Paddy and the man nodded. *"Well then, dinnae be sae daft,"* replied Paddy. Soon after recruiting, Crossan was selected for the Scottish League XI with teammates Peter Nellies, Jamie Low, and Harry Graham.

On 18 June 1915, 1,100 officers and men, with McCrae on horseback, marched down the Mound, led by Willie Duguid's pipers, and the scene was filmed for release in the cinemas. The battalion congregated on the southbound platform at Edinburgh Waverley railway station. McCrae was saying his goodbyes to directors Leishman, Hogge, and Rawson. Manager John McCartney and Chairman Furst were attending to the players. Currie was a sergeant; Low, Gracie, Findlay, and Briggs were corporals. Boyd, Ellis, Wattie, and Crossan remained privates. Alice Wattie was there for her brother and her fiancé. Crossan would not let go of her hand. As the carriages began to move, carrying the 16th off to war, McCartney later poignantly wrote, *"I heard the cheering start again. The finest men I ever knew had gone."*

After the battalions first stint on the front-line near Bois Grenier, Crossan wrote to McCartney on 10 February 1916, about his solution to the stalemate on the Western Front. *"I think instead of fighting we should take the Fritzes on at football. I am certain we would do it on them."*

On the morning of 1 July, the Hearts boys sat close to each other on the fire-step, the raised platform in the trench for conducting defensive firing from the parapet. Crossan sat quietly. Their objective was the village of La Boisselle near Contalmaison. Crossan was part of Cole's C Company and by late morning they had remained largely intact. Cole ordered a charge out of the sunken road and carnage followed as they ran into a nest of German machine-guns. Ellis, Hawthorn, Hazeldean, and Currie were all scythed down in the hail of bullets. Crossan was racing forward beside two Suffolks when a shell exploded in front of them. The Suffolks were obliterated and Crossan was posted missing.

A week later, on 8 July, Crossan miraculously reappeared from No Man's Land back at Battalion HQ at Henencourt. He had been buried by the explosion and regained consciousness the following morning to find that the two Suffolks lay dead beside him. It took him three days to crawl back to safety. Some English lads had directed him to a dressing station, where he was pronounced fit to return to his unit. He remained concussed for a week and suffered hearing loss for several months. On 10 July, Contalmaison was finally taken by the British.

Back on active service, he was hit in the leg by shrapnel near Bazentin on 9 August 1916, as the Battle of the Somme raged on. The leg was marked for amputation but was saved after being operated on by a German POW surgeon. By the middle of November, Crossan was recovering in a military hospital in Stourbridge, near Birmingham, where he was visited by Alice Wattie. He wrote to McCartney that he expected to be kicking a ball 'quite soon'. After recovering,

Crossan was transferred to the 4th Royal Scots (Lothian Regiment) to serve in the Sinai and Palestine Campaign and he was in action during the Battle of Jerusalem in December 1917. He was posted back to the Western Front, the 4th Royal Scots landing in Marseilles on 17 April 1918 and he was severely gassed on 26 August, during an attack on Hende-court. Private 18998 Patrick Crossan was awarded the Victory and British War medals.

John Veitch visited him in an Edinburgh convalescent home on the evening of Armistice Day. Veitch asked Crossan what his intentions were and the player looked over to Arthur's Seat, stating: "First, I'm going to run up yon wee hill, then I'm going back to play for Hearts." He returned to Hearts after the war and featured in another six full seasons, receiving two benefit games and bringing his total number of competitive appearances to over 300, before being released on a free transfer in 1925, aged 31. Crossan signed for Leith Athletic in August 1925. He scored against his old club Hearts in a 7–1 defeat on 19 August 1925.

After he retired from football, he opened Paddy's Bar at 49 Rose Street in Edinburgh city centre. Patrick James Crossan, 33, a wine and spirit merchant, married Mary Alice Wattie, 36, a cashier and the sister of his old comrade Harry, both of 12 Marchmont Road, Morningside, Edinburgh, on 21 January 1926 in a civil ceremony at 3 York Place, Edinburgh by warrant of the Sheriff Substitute of Lothians and Peebles. Patrick Crossan died of tuberculosis in 1933 and was buried in Mount Vernon Cemetery, Edinburgh. Paddy's Bar is still a public house institution on Rose Street to this day.

Paddy's parents - Edward Crossan and Bridget Nicholas

Paddy's father Edward Crossan was born on 4 September 1867 at Waringstown, County Down, Ireland to father Michael Crossan, a flax mill hand, and mother Isabella Morgan. Paddy's mother Bridget Nicholas (or Nicklas) was born on 11 April 1866 in Blackburn, Livingston, Linlithgowshire, to father Michael Nicholas, a labourer at a chemical works, and mother Mary Jane Welsh (or Walshe). In 1881, Bridget, 14, a general servant, resided at 17 Graham Street, Addiewell, West Calder, with her father Michael Nicholas, 39, a labourer in a shale oil works, mother Mary, 37, a domestic servant, and her siblings.

Edward Crossan, 21, a foundry labourer, of 15 Collier Street, Johnstone, Renfrewshire, married Bridget Nicholas, 21, a wick mill hand, of 18 Dimity Street, Johnstone, on 22 February 1889 at St Margaret's RC Church, Johnstone. The wedding was conducted by Fr James Rochead, RC clergyman; the best man was Andrew Keenan and the best maid was Mary J O'Carron. Edward and Bridget had six known children; in Glasgow, John (b. ~1889), in Addiewell, Patrick (b. 21 May 1891), Isabella (b. ~1893), Mary (b. ~1894), in Johnstone, Michael (b. ~1896) and Edward (b. ~1899). Son Patrick James Crossan was born on 21 May 1891 at 7 Baker Street, Addiewell, West Calder to father Edward Crossan, a fireman in the mines, and mother Bridget Nicholas.

In 1901, Edward Crossan, 33, a shale oil works labourer, resided at 3 Simpson Street, Addiewell, West Calder, with wife Bridget, 35, children John, 11, Patrick, 9, Isabella, 8,

Mary, 7, all scholars, Michael, 5, and Edward, 2. Edward, an oil worker, and Bridget were both dead by 1926.

Paddy's paternal grandparents - Michael Crossan and Isabella Morgan

Paddy's paternal grandfather Michael Crossan (or Crossen) was born to father Bernard Crossan and his grandmother Isabella Morgan, aka Bella, was born to father Thomas Morgan, both around 1840 in County Down, Ireland. Michael Crossan, a flax mill hand, married Bella Morgan on 4 November 1866 in Banbridge, County Down and they had three known children in Waringstown, County Down; Edward (b. 4 September 1867), and likely twins Rose Ann and Mary Jane (b. 19 May 1870).

Waringstown lies in Donaghcloney parish and was named after Cromwellian Englishman William Waring who purchased the lands in 1659, following the Irish Confederate Wars. Waring's son Samuel brought over skilled Huguenot Flemish weavers and Waringstown became a centre of damask and linen weaving. Michael Crossan, a flax mill hand, was still alive in 1889, although, his wife Isabella was dead by then.

Paddy's maternal grandparents - Michael McNicholas and Mary Jane Welsh

Paddy's maternal grandfather Michael McNicholas (or Nicholas or McNichol) was born around 1843 in Ireland to father Michael McNicholas, a labourer, and mother Sarah

McDonald. Many Irish immigrants tended to anglicize their names by dropping the 'Mac' and 'O' prefixes. Paddy's grandmother Mary Jane Welsh (or Walshe) was born around 1843 in Ireland to father John Welsh, a labourer, and mother Bridget MacIntyre.

Michael McNicholas, 22, a railway labourer, married Mary Walshe, 22, an agricultural labourer, who signed with their 'x' marks, both of Blackburn, Linlithgowshire, on 20 June 1865 at Bathgate Roman Catholic Church. The wedding was conducted by Fr Andrew Boland, RC clergyman, and the sponsor was John Coyne. Fr Boland also recorded the marriage in the CPRs for Bathgate RC Church as follows:-

Michael McNicholas Mary Walshe were after due proclamation of banns, married at Bathgate Catholic Church June 20th '65 by me: Boland: Witnesses Anthony Laing Catherine Coyne

Michael and Mary had six known children; in Blackburn, Bridget (b. 11 April 1866), Patrick (b. ~1868), Annie (b. ~1871), Mary (b. ~1874), Maggie (b. ~1876), and in Addiewell, Michael (b. ~1879). Daughter Bridget Nicholas was born on 11 April 1866 in Blackburn, Livingston, Linlithgowshire, to father Michael Nicholas, a labourer at a chemical works, and mother Mary Jane Welsh. This was almost certainly the same Bathgate Chemical Works where Jimmy Boyd's grandfather Archibald Renwick also worked.

In 1881, Michael Nicholas, 39, a labourer in a shale oil works, resided at 17 Graham Street, Addiewell, West Calder, with wife Mary, 37, a domestic servant, children Bridget, 14, a general servant, Patrick, 13, Annie, 10, Mary, 7, Maggie,

5, and Michael, 2. Michael and Mary were both still alive in 1889.

Paddy's paternal great-grandfather - Bernard Crossan

Paddy's paternal great-grandfather Bernard Crossan was born around 1815 most likely in County Down, Ireland. Bernard Crossan had a son Michael (b. ~1840) in County Down. Bernard was still alive in 1866 in County Down.

Paddy's paternal great-grandfather – Thomas Morgan

Paddy's other paternal great-grandfather Thomas Morgan was born around 1815 most likely in County Down, Ireland. Thomas Morgan had a daughter Isabella, aka Bella (b. ~1840) in County Down. Thomas was still alive in 1866 in County Down.

Paddy's maternal great-grandparents – Michael McNicholas and Sarah McDonald

Paddy's maternal great-grandparents Michael McNicholas and Sarah McDonald were born around 1820 in Ireland. Michael, a labourer, and Sarah had a son Michael (b. ~1843) in Ireland. Michael and Sarah were still alive in 1865 in Ireland, having lived through the Irish Potato Famine.

Paddy's maternal great-grandparents
John Welsh and Bridget MacIntyre

Paddy's other maternal great-grandparents John Welsh and Bridget MacIntyre were born around 1820 in Ireland. John, a labourer, and Bridget had a daughter Mary Jane (b. ~1843) in Ireland. John, a labourer, was still alive in 1865 in Ireland, although, his wife Bridget was dead by then.

Chapter 9

Norman Findlay
Corporal,
16th Battalion Royal Scots

Norman Findlay (1890 – 1949)

Norman Morrison Findlay, named after his Stornoway-born grandfather, was born in the 1st Quarter 1890 in Walker-on-Tyne, Longbenton, Tynemouth, Northumberland, to Scottish-born parents, father Robert Findlay and mother Margaret Morrison as registered in Volume 10b Page 257. In 1891, Norman, 1, resided in Swan Street, Walker, Longbenton, with his father Robert Findlay, 37, mother Margaret, 34, and his other siblings. In 1901, Norman, 11, at school, still resided at Swan Street, Walker, with his father Robert Findlay, 47, a ship's riveter, mother Margaret, 43, and his other siblings.

Findlay was a professional goalkeeper who played for Hearts and Coventry City. His football career started out with Blyth Spartans, when, in 1914, he was signed by John McCartney to play for Hearts, making only one appearance before war broke out. Although he remained on Hearts books until 1919, he made guest appearances for his local team Walker Celtic in 1915–16. In 1921 he was signed by Coventry City and although he remained at Highfield Road until 1926, he only managed nine appearances in goal for the Sky Blues.

On 25 November 1914, one of eleven Hearts players, Findlay, in the second team squad at that time, enlisted as a Corporal in McCrae's 16th Battalion, the Royal Scots. On 18 June 1915, Findlay was on the southbound train, along with 1,100 men of the 16th, cheered off from Edinburgh Waverley.

Norman Findlay never got the chance to join his teammates in France. A ship's carpenter to trade, he was released from the army in September 1916 to work in protected employment in the Tyneside shipyards, at Swan & Hunter's Wallsend Shipyard, helping to build warships. After his spell with Coventry City ended, he moved to Isleworth in Middlesex, working to repair barges on the River Thames. He married wife Grace Warby in the 3rd Quarter 1933 in Brentford, Middlesex as registered in Volume 3a Page 646. Another of McCrae's succumbing to the 'curse of the old 16th', Norman Morrison Findlay, only 59, died in the spring of 1949 as registered in Ealing, Middlesex.

Norman's parents -
Robert Findlay and Margaret Morrison

Norman's father Robert Findlay (or Finlay) was born on Christmas Day, 25 December 1853 in Govan, Glasgow, Lanarkshire, to father David Findlay, a spirit dealer, and mother Catherine Hamilton. The birth is registered in the OPRs for the parish of Govan (Ref: 646/3/154) as follows:-

1853: Govan Parish Register of Births: December 25:
Robert lawful son to David Findlay & Catherine
Hamilton

Norman's mother Margaret Morrison (or Morison), aka Maggie, was born on 14 December 1856 at Keith Street, Stornoway, Isle of Lewis, Ross-shire, to father Norman Morrison, a shoemaker, and mother Ann McIntosh. The birth was registered by Margaret's father Norman Morrison, who signed with his 'x' mark, on 22 December 1856 at the Stornoway Registry Office.

After leaving school Robert Findlay became an apprentice riveter in the fast-expanding and world-renowned Govan shipyards, in Messrs Alexander Stephen and Sons' Linthouse Shipyard. In March 1881, Robert Findlay, 27, a riveter, lodged at the home of Malcolm Morrison, 40, a ship's carpenter in Alexander Stephen's shipyard, at 35 James Place, Govan. Malcolm Morrison was the uncle of Margaret Morrison and through him Maggie and Robert met and fell in love. Robert Findlay, 27, a riveter, of 14 Greenhaugh Street, Govan, married Maggie Morrison, 24, a domestic servant, of 35 James Place, Govan, on 19 August 1881. The wedding was conducted by Rev Allan Cameron, minister of Govan Free Church of Scotland; the best man was David Findlay, Robert's brother, and the best maid was Christina Morrison, Maggie's cousin.

Robert and Maggie had seven known children in Lancashire and Northumberland; in Barrow-in-Furness, David (b. 1st Quarter 1883), Anne, aka Annie (b. ~1885), in Walker-on-Tyne, Catherine, aka Kate (b. ~1888,), Norman Morrison (b. 1st Quarter 1890), Robert (b. ~1894), Jane (b.

~1897) and Margaret (b. ~1904). By early 1883, Robert was working for James Ramsden's Barrow Shipbuilding Company in Lancashire, which specialised in naval warships. In 1897 it was bought over by the mighty Vickers Armstrong Company, still currently involved in the construction of warships for the Royal Navy as Vickers Shipbuilding and Engineering Ltd.

Back in Glasgow, on 3 July 1883, the newly-built SS Daphne was being side-launched, as was the common practice at that time, from Alexander Stephen's Linthouse yard into the River Clyde. Again, it was the practice for shipyard workers, men and boys, to continue working on board completing the internal fittings during the launch, and around 200 ship's carpenters, joiners, plumbers, caulkers, and boilermakers carried on with their jobs as the Daphne slid down the oiled slipways. One of the men aboard the Daphne was ship's carpenter Malcolm Morrison, Maggie's uncle.

The heavy chains which acted as the checking apparatus failed and as the Daphne reached the water it toppled over onto its side, throwing men and boys into the Clyde. A joiner named Kinnaird, who survived, later reported:-

"I was busily engaged on the deck, and felt the vessel moving on the ways, and nothing occurred until she had taken the river. Then an extraordinary scene happened, and tremendous shouts arose from those on board. I felt the vessel toppling over to the right and in a moment every person on board was hurled into the water. The shrieks and cries were terrible...I believe that over two hundred people were in the vessel. I cannot

possibly describe the heart-breaking scenes which I witnessed."

One hundred and twenty four men and boys died in the Clyde's worst shipbuilding disaster, including Maggie's uncle, *'Malcolm Morrison, 45, a carpenter, 35 James Place, Govan, married'*. In a Register of Corrected Entries it is recorded that 'Malcolm Morrison, 44, a carpenter, Male, died on 3rd July 1883, in River Clyde at or near Linthouse near Glasgow, Usual Residence James Place, Govan. Cause of death, drowning (Accident at launch of S.S. Daphne). Burial Place & Undertaker, Craigton Cemetery, Jenkins, Govan. Certified on 2nd August 1883 by James N Hart, Procurator Fiscal'.

Following a Fatal Accident Inquiry it was recommended that only limited personnel would remain on board at a ship's launch and the practice of side-launching was generally phased out in favour of longitudinal-launching on the Clyde. There are two SS Daphne Memorials to the dead, one in Elder Park, Govan and the other in Victoria Park, Whiteinch. The SS Daphne was re-floated, repaired and relaunched as SS Rose.

Robert and Maggie's son Norman Morrison Findlay was born in the 1st Quarter 1890 in Walker-on-Tyne, Longbenton, Tynemouth, Northumberland. Robert was employed in the naval architectural firm Swan & Hunter Shipbuilding Company in nearby Wallsend, founded in 1880 by George Hunter and the widow of Charles Sheridan Swan of the Wallsend Shipbuilding Company. C S Swan, who died in 1879, was the son of farmer William Swan of Old Walker, Longbenton, and Swan Street is named after him. Swan Hunter still currently build and maintain warships for the Royal Navy.

In 1891, Robert Findlay, 37, a shipyard riveter, resided in Swan Street, Walker, with wife Margaret, 34, children David, 8, Anne, 6, Catherine, 3, and Norman, 1. In 1901, Robert Findlay, 47, a ship's riveter, still resided in Swan Street, Walker, with wife Margaret, 43, children David, 18, Annie, 16, Kate, 13, Norman, 11, Robert, 7, and Jane, 4. In 1911, Robert Findlay, 56, a ship's riveter, still resided in Walker, Longbenton, with wife Margaret, 53, children Annie, 26, Robert, 17, Jane, 14, and Margaret, 7.

Norman's paternal grandparents -
David Findlay and Catherine Hamilton

Norman's paternal grandfather David Findlay (or Finlay) was born about 1826 in Paisley, Renfrewshire to father Robert Findlay, a cotton weaver, and mother Janet Ramsay. His grandmother Catherine Hamilton was born around 1825 in Govan, Glasgow to father John Hamilton, a grocer, and mother Jean Park. David Findlay, a spirit dealer, married Catherine Hamilton, both parishioners in Govan, on 5 June 1851. The marriage is recorded in the OPRs for the parish of Govan (Ref: 646/3/273) as follows:-

> *1851: [Booked] May 24: [Married] June 5: David*
> *Findlay & Catherine Hamilton: [His parish] Govan:*
> *[Her parish] Govan*

David and Catherine had five known children in Govan; Jane (b. ~1852), Robert (b. 25 December 1853), John W (b. ~1856), David (b. ~1858) and Catherine (b. ~1859). Son Robert

Findlay was born on Christmas Day, 25 December 1853 in Govan, Glasgow. In 1861, David Findlay, 35, was the inn keeper of the Sheep Head Inn, Renfrew Road, Hyndford, Govan, with wife Catherine, 36, children Jane, 9, Robert, 7, both scholars, John W, 5, Catherine, 2, and Helen Boyd, 24, a general servant.

The Sheep Head Inn was an old established tavern and the name is derived from the symbol of Govan, the sheep's head, which is annually paraded at the ancient traditional Govan Fair. It is based on a late 18th century legend that tells of a minister who forbade his housemaid to marry a young Govanite lad. The pair eloped and were irregularly married to the fury of the minister. Legend states that the local Govan folk rose up against the minister and beheaded his prize sheep or ram and paraded it through the streets of Govan.

Shortly after the 1861 census David fell seriously ill. David Findlay, only 37, a spirit dealer, died on 5 May 1862 at the Sheep Head Inn, Govan of Bright's disease of the kidneys and hepatitis, for six months, as certified by Dr R B Hislop MD. The death was registered by David's father-in-law John Hamilton on 6 May 1862 at the Govan Registry Office. Bright's disease, now called nephritis, is a hereditary disease which can be triggered by a urinary tract infection, such as, in David's case, hepatitis.

David's death left his wife Catherine with five young children and it was financially imperative for her to take another husband or face being put into the Govan Combination Poorhouse. Catherine married her second husband James Todd, a dyke builder, but the marriage was fairly short-lived. Catherine Todd, previously Findlay nee Hamilton, only 46, died on 29 October 1870 at 43 Hamilton

Street, Govan of that dreaded Victorian killer, consumption (pulmonary tuberculosis), as certified by Dr A Macfie Smith MD. The death was registered by Catherine's daughter Jane Findlay, still only 18, on 1 November 1870 at the Govan Registry Office.

Norman's maternal grandparents – Norman Morrison and Ann McIntosh

Norman's maternal grandfather Norman Morrison (or Morison) was born around 1836 in Stornoway, Isle of Lewis to father Kenneth Morrison, a master shoemaker, and mother Isabella Macaulay. His grandmother Ann McIntosh (or Macintosh), aka Annie, was born around 1835 also in Stornoway to father Duncan McIntosh, a general labourer, and mother Christina MacLennan.

Norman Morrison, a shoemaker, married Ann McIntosh around 1855 in Stornoway and they had five known children there; Margaret (b. 14 December 1856), Bell Ann (b. ~1867), George N (b. ~1869), Macintosh (b. ~1875) and Kenneth (b. ~1879). Daughter Margaret Morrison, aka Maggie, was born on 14 December 1856 at Keith Street, Stornoway. The birth was registered by Margaret's father Norman Morrison, a shoemaker, who signed with his 'x' mark, on 22 December 1856 at the Stornoway Registry Office.

In 1881, when daughter Margaret had moved to Govan in Glasgow to work as a domestic servant, Norman Morrison, 46, a shoemaker, resided at No.34 Inaclete, Stornoway, with wife Ann, 47, children Bell Ann, 14, George N, 12,

Macintosh, 6, all scholars, and Kenneth, 2. The Morrison family were all Gaelic-spoken.

Norman Morrison, 73, a master shoemaker, died on 14 May 1909 at 12 Newton Street, Stornoway of arteriosclerosis and cerebral softening as certified by Dr Murdoch Mackenzie LRCP&S Edin. Norman's death was registered by his son-in-law William Rudland, of Francis Street, Stornoway, on 19 May 1909 at the Stornoway Registry Office. Norman's widow, Ann Morrison nee McIntosh, 79, died on 6 April 1914 at 12 Newton Street, Stornoway of chronic bronchitis and pulmonary congestion as certified by Dr J Pringle Tolmie LRCP&S Edin. The death was again registered by son-in-law William Rudland, of 42 Francis Street, on 11 April 1914 at the Stornoway Registry Office.

Just ten weeks later, on 28 June 1914, the Archduke Franz Ferdinand of Austria was assassinated by student Gavril Principe in Sarajevo. This was the key event that triggered the outbreak of the Great War on 28 July 1914, and into the conflict, which Ann's grandson, Norman Morrison Findlay found himself compelled to enlist with McCrae's Battalion.

The Isle of Lewis and Harris was to pay a high price in WW1, losing 6,000 young men from a population of 30,000, but the greatest tragedy in the island's history came just 7 weeks after the Armistice was signed. On New Years' Day, 1 January 1919, the steam yacht Iolare tried to enter Storno-way harbour in a gale. On board the overcrowded yacht were 284 men returning from the war to celebrate the New Year with their loved ones. Apparently blown off course, the Iolare struck rocks and quickly began sinking. Within sight of Stornoway harbour and watched in terror by their waiting relatives, 205 men drowned, including 174 Lewis men, 7

Harris men and other crewmen. It is the worst maritime disaster in the island's history.

Norman's paternal great-grandparents - Robert Findlay and Janet Ramsay

Norman's paternal great-grandfather Robert Findlay and his great-grandmother Janet Ramsay were born about 1795 possibly in Paisley, Renfrewshire. Robert Findlay, a cotton weaver, married Janet Ramsay and they had a known son David (b. ~1826) in Paisley, Renfrewshire. At that time, Paisley was becoming a world-renowned centre for textile weaving, particularly, due to the popularity of the intricate paisley-pattern. Robert, a cotton weaver, and Janet were both dead by 1862.

Norman's paternal great-grandparents - John Hamilton and Jean Park

Norman's other paternal great-grandfather John Hamilton and his great-grandmother Jean Park were probably born about 1795 in Glasgow. John Hamilton, a grocer, married Jean Park and they had a known daughter Catherine (b. ~1825) in Govan, Glasgow. On 6 May 1862, John Hamilton registered the death of his son-in-law David Findlay at the Govan Registry Office. John, a grocer, was still alive in 1870, although, his wife Jean was dead by then.

Norman's maternal great-grandparents – Kenneth Morrison and Isabella Macaulay

Norman's maternal great-grandfather Kenneth Morrison (or Morison) and his great-grandmother Isabella Macaulay were both born about 1810 in Stornoway, Isle of Lewis. Kenneth Morrison, a master shoemaker, married Isabella Macaulay and they had two known sons; Norman (b. ~1836) and Malcolm (b. ~1839) in Stornoway. In 1837 *Pigot's Trade Directory*, Kenneth Morrison is listed under *'Boot and Shoemakers'* with a shop in Keith Street, Stornoway.

On 19 July 1883 at the Govan Registry Office, Kenneth, a master shoemaker, then of 12 Newton Street, Stornoway, had the sad duty of registering the death of his son Malcolm, a shipwright journeyman, who had died on 3 July 1883 of drowning at the Linthouse Shipyard in Govan, when the launch of the SS Daphne went catastrophically wrong. Kenneth, a shoemaker, and Isabella were both dead by 1909.

Norman's maternal great-grandparents – Duncan McIntosh and Christina McLennan

Norman's other maternal great-grandfather Duncan McIntosh (or Macintosh) and his great-grandmother Christina McLennan, aka Christian, were both born around 1810 in Stornoway, Isle of Lewis. Duncan McIntosh, a general labourer, married Christina MacLennan and they had a known daughter Ann, aka Annie, (b. ~1835) in Stornoway. Duncan, a general labourer, and Christina were both dead by 1914.

Chapter 10

James Frew
Private,
16th Battalion Royal Scots

James Frew (1891 – 1967)

James Hearty Frew was born on 21 May 1891 at Ivy [Ives] Cottage, Kinghorn, Fife, to father Archibald Frew, an iron driller, and mother Catherine Hearty. Jimmy's youth career in football started with Kilsyth Emmet, followed by Alloa Athletic and Newcastle City. He signed for Hearts as a left back in season 1912–13 and remained on Hearts books until 1920, in total making 35 appearances for the Gorgie club either side of the war. In June 1920 he was sold to Leeds United, and in July 1924, following serious injury, he transferred to a player-coaching post at Bradford City.

Jimmy Frew, a second-team member, was among the eleven players who enlisted on 25 November 1914 in McCrae's Battalion in Edinburgh. On Friday 26 February 1915, Jimmy Frew, 23, of 21 Westfield Road, Edinburgh, married Jeanie Catherine Campbell, of 235 Dalry Road, Edinburgh. The wedding was conducted by Rev J Struthers Symington MA, minister of Fountainbridge United Free Church. The best man was teammate Sergeant Annan Buchan Ness and the best maid was Jimmy's sister, Kitty Hearty Frew. Frew left the 16th Battalion in January 1916, transferring as Gunner, later Staff Sergeant, 307245 in McCrae's son's battery of the Royal Garrison Artillery. In May 1916, Frew played one unofficial wartime international for Scotland alongside teammate Willie Wilson. Staff Sergeant 307245 James H Frew Royal Garrison Artillery was awarded the Victory and British War medals.

Jimmy Frew joined Leeds United after the war, making 96 appearances between 1920 and 1924, including three FA Cup games. He transferred to Bradford City with 48 appearances between 1924 and 1926. His career was curtailed by injury and he opened a sports outfitters in Leeds, combining the business with a second career as a trainer, including his coaching post at Bradford City. Frew rose through the ranks to become the FA's chief coach in West Yorkshire. He encouraged the legendary late Jack Charlton, the England World Cup hero in 1966, among others, to consider their first moves into football management. James Hearty Frew, 74, died on 27 April 1967 in Leeds, Yorkshire.

Jimmy's parents - Archibald Frew and Catherine Hearty

Jimmy's paternal grandfather Archibald Frew was born around 1854 in Coatdyke, Old Monkland, Lanarkshire, to father Daniel Frew, a railway porter, and mother Margaret Stirling. Jimmy's grandmother Catherine Hearty (or Harty) was born on 19 May 1858 at Harbour Place, Burntisland, Fife, to father William Hearty, a coal labourer in a shipyard, and mother Barbara Robertson. In 1861, Archibald, 7, a scholar, resided at South Hill Street, Burntisland, with father Daniel Frew, 38, a railway porter, mother Margaret, 39, and his siblings. In 1871, with her mother Barbara dead and her father William remarried, Catherine Hearty, only 13, a flax factory worker, boarded at Nethergate, Kinghorn, with Barbara Page, 39, a former flax worker.

Archibald Frew, 22, a shipyard labourer, married Catherine Hearty, 19, a mill worker, both of Kinghorn, Fife, on 5 July 1877. The wedding was conducted by Rev William Jardine Dobie, minister of Kinghorn; the best man was Thomas Hillock and the best maid was Margaret Frew, Archibald's sister. Archie and Catherine had seven known children; in Kinghorn, Archibald (b. ~1878), William (b. ~1880), Daniel (b. ~1882), Barbara (b. ~1884), Sydney (b. ~1889), James (b. 21 May 1891), and in Leith, Margaret aka Maggie (b. ~1887).

In 1891, Archibald Frew, 34, a shipyard driller, resided at Ivy Cottage, Bruce Street, Kinghorn, with wife Catherine, 32, heavily pregnant with son James, children Archibald, 13, a storekeeper's assistant, William, 11, Daniel, 9, Barbara, 7, all scholars, Maggie, 4, and Sydney, 2. Son James Hearty Frew was born on 21 May 1891 at Ivy [Ives] Cottage, Bruce Street, Kinghorn, Fife. Archibald Frew, an iron driller, and wife Catherine were both still alive in 1915.

Jimmy's paternal grandparents - Daniel Frew and Margaret Stirling

Jimmy's paternal grandfather Daniel Frew was born on 12 March 1820 in Coatdyke, Old Monkland, Lanarkshire to father Daniel Frew, a coal master, and mother Mary McNair. Jimmy's grandmother Margaret Stirling was born around 1822 in Edinburgh, Midlothian to father Peter Stirling, a horse dealer, and mother Helen Watt. In 1841, Daniel, 20, an engineer, resided in Coatdyke, Old Monkland, with his father Daniel Frew, 45, a coal master of independent means, mother Mary, 50, and his siblings. In 1841, Margaret, 20, resided at 118 Princes Street, St George's, Edinburgh, with her father Peter Stirling, 45, a horse dealer, mother Helen, 40, and her siblings.

Daniel Frew, a blacksmith merchant, in Airdrie, New Monkland, married Margaret Stirling, of 52 Broughton Street, St Mary's, Edinburgh on 27 August 1846. The marriage is recorded, as was customary, in the OPRs for the respective parishes of Coatbridge or Old Monkland (Ref: 652/3/266) and St Mary's, Edinburgh (Ref: 685/1/68/204) as follows:-

1846: July 19: Daniel Frew, Blacksmith, Coatdyke, this parish & Margaret Stirling, parish of St Mary's, Edinburgh: 2 days

1846: Edinburgh 13th July: (Proclaimed 12th July 1846): Daniel Frew, merchant parish of Airdrie, and Margaret Stirling, residing No.52 Broughton Street, Saint Mary's Parish, daughter of Peter Stirling, Horse dealer, have been three times proclaimed in order to Marriage in the Parish church of St Mary's and no objections having been offered. Married at Edinburgh on 27th day of August 1846 by the Revd Dr John Brown of Broughton Place.

There is a sizeable gap between the proclamation of banns on 12 July 1846 and the actual marriage on 27 August 1846. This is almost certainly because Daniel's father, the coal master at Kipps Colliery, died on 5 August 1846, interrupting the marriage preparations. When his father's estate (valued circa £50k currently) was settled on 5 February 1847, Daniel, recorded as the smith at Coatdyke Colliery, received a quarter share. With this money Daniel and Margaret moved to Edinburgh to further his ambitions as an engineer.

Daniel and Margaret had seven known children; in Edinburgh, Daniel (b. ~1847), Peter (b. ~1849), James (b. 25 January 1851), Helen Watt Burns (b. 11 August 1852), in Coatdyke, Archibald (b. ~1854), and in Burntisland, Margaret (b. ~1858) and David G C Frew (b. ~1860). The following births are recorded in the OPRs for Bread Street United Presbyterian Church (Ref: CH3/112/1/214 & 228) as follows:-

1851: [No.] 1697: Daniel Frew, Engineer, residing 6 Tollcross & Margaret Stirling his Spouse, a son James, born & baptized the 25th January 1851 By the Revd Mr Millar: George Barbour Session Clerk

1852: [No.] 1801: Daniel Frew, Engineer, residing 9 Elbe Street, Leith & Margaret Stirling his Spouse, a daughter Helen Watt Burns, born 11th August & baptized November 1852 By the Revd R D Duncan: Thomas Leitch Session Clerk

Son Archibald Frew was born around 1854 in Coatdyke, Old Monkland, to father Daniel Frew, now working as a railway porter, and mother Margaret Stirling. It would appear that Daniel's career as a skilled blacksmith, coal merchant and mining engineer had ended by this juncture in the mid-1850s and he was by then working as a more humble railway porter with the North British Railway Company, moving his family to Fife. In 1861, Daniel Frew, 38, a railway porter, resided at South Hill Street, Burntisland, with wife Margaret, 39, children Daniel, 14, a message boy, Peter, 12, James, 10, Helen, 9, Archibald, 7, all scholars, Margaret, 3, and David G C, 1.

Daniel and wife Margaret were both still alive in 1888, although, Daniel Frew, a railway porter, 67, died on 6 October 1888 in the Fife & Kinross Asylum, Cupar of disease of the spinal cord, atrophy and degeneration for 27 years, also phthisis pulmonalis (tuberculosis) for several years, as certified by Dr A H Turnbull MD. Daniel, the son of a successful and upwardly mobile coal master, had been making the most of the economic opportunities presented by the Industrial Revolution. However, Daniel's degenerative disease is the likely explanation for his own promising engineering career ending up with him only able to hold down the position of a railway porter.

Jimmy's maternal grandparents - William Hearty and Barbara Robertson

Jimmy's maternal grandfather William Hearty (or Harty) was born around 1833 in Ireland to father Thomas Hearty, a gardener, and mother Janet Templeton. Jimmy's grandmother Barbara Robertson was born around 1835 possibly in Fife. Daughter Catherine Hearty was born on 19 May 1858 at Harbour Place, Burntisland, Fife, to father William Hearty, a coal labourer in a shipyard, and mother Barbara Robertson. William and Barbara also had a son James born around 1859 in Burntisland. By 1871, Barbara was dead and William Hearty married a second wife named Ann, possibly a common-law wife. Daughter Catherine, 13, had left the family home and was boarding at Nethergate in Kinghorn.

In 1881, William Hearty, 48, a labourer in a shipyard, resided at 11 Abden House, Kinghorn, with Dunfermline-born wife Ann, 49, a millworker. William must have been down on his luck, as Abden House was part of the Kirkcaldy and Abbotshall Combination Poorhouse. William Hearty, stated as 50, but more likely 54, a general labourer, of 20 Wilkie Place, North Leith, Midlothian, married third wife Mary Ann Lyall nee Trail, 47, widow of Robert Lyall, a ship steward, of 12 Wilkie Place, North Leith, on 25 October 1887 at Mary Ann's home. The wedding was conducted by Rev James Stevenson, minister of North Leith United Presbyterian Church; the best man was Donald McLeod and the best maid was Robina Low.

William Hearty, 77, a shipyard labourer, died on 17 March 1902 at North Leith Hospital of apoplexy, for 3 days, as certified by Dr J M Johnston MB. The death was registered by his son James Hearty, of 2 Cameron Place, Clydebank, on 19 March 1902 at North Leith Registry Office. Son James obviously kept up some minimal contact with his father William over the years, however, he was unable to state his grandparents' names or his father's home address in Leith. William's son James Hearty, 77, a ship's plater in the

Clydebank shipyards, died on 3 April 1938 of a cerebral haemorrhage at 39 Barns Street, Clydebank.

Jimmy's paternal grandparents - Daniel Frew and Mary McNair

Jimmy's paternal great-grandfather Daniel Frew was born around 1795 and his great-grandmother Mary McNair was born around 1791, both in Old Monkland, Lanarkshire. Daniel Frew married Mary McNair on 28 June 1811 in Old Monkland. The marriage is recorded in the OPRs for Coatbridge or Old Monkland (Ref: 652/1/451) as follows:-

1811: June 28: Also Daniel Frew and Mary McNair both in this parish to be proclaimed on the two following Sabbaths ~

Daniel, a coal master, and Mary had seven known children in Old Monkland; Agnes (b. ~1812), James (b. ~1814), George (b. ~1816), Bethia Rymer (b. ~1818), Daniel (b. 12 March 1820), Thomas (b. ~1826) and Archibald (b. ~1829). Daniel Frew was a coal master and partner in Messrs Frew at the coal pit of Kipps Byre near Airdrie. A dreadful accident occurred there on 8 June 1831, which was reported three days later in *The Scotsman*:-

About 6 o'clock on Wednesday morning, an explosion of fire damp [methane gas] took place in a coal pit at Keppisbyre, in a neighbourhood of Airdrie, belonging to the Messrs Frew, by which a lad about 15 years of age, of the name of Peter Campbell, lost his life, and

Peter Gentles, Alexander MacLaren, and James Young,
were most dreadfully scorched and bruised.

It was reported on 27 June 1831 in The Caledonian Mercury that only Alexander MacLaren survived the accident and, in total, four lives were lost.

In 1841, Daniel Frew, 45, a coal master of independent means, resided in Coatdyke, Old Monkland, with wife Mary, 50, children Bethia, 20, Daniel, 20, an engineer, Thomas, 15, a banker, Archibald, 12, and a female servant Ann McKenzie, 20. Daniel Frew, a coal master in Coatdyke, died on 5 August 1846 and he left a will with an estate valued at £561 4s 3d (approximately £50k currently). The will was signed by son Thomas Frew, a banker, and Henry Glassford Bell, Sheriff Substitute for Lanarkshire, in favour of Daniel's children Thomas, George, a blacksmith at Kipps, Daniel, a blacksmith at Coatdyke, and Bethia, married to James Crichton, an Airdrie grocer.

Henry Glassford Bell (1803–1874) was born in Glasgow to James Bell, an advocate, and he was a well-known lawyer, poet and historian. He rose to become sheriff of Lanarkshire in 1867. Among his written works is a preface, which he wrote to Bell & Bain's 1865 edition of the works of Shakespeare.

After Daniel's death and by the 1850s, the coal pit at Kipps Colliery had become part of the ever-expanding William Baird and Company, which would build a worker's institute at nearby Gartsherrie, Old Monkland.

Jimmy's paternal great-grandparents – Peter Stirling and Helen Watt

Jimmy's other paternal great-grandfather Peter Stirling was born around 1795 and great-grandmother Helen Watt was born around 1797 to father John Watt, a blacksmith. In 1816 Peter Stirling was a gentleman's servant residing at No.23 Jamaica Street, New Town, Edinburgh. The mews construction complete with stables at 23 Jamaica Street is a preserved historic listed building in Edinburgh New Town.

Peter Stirling, a gentleman's servant of No.23 Jamaica Street, Edinburgh, married Helen Watt, of No.240 Water of Leith, Edinburgh, the daughter of John Watt, a blacksmith, on 29 May 1816. The marriage is recorded in the OPRs for St Cuthbert's (Ref: 685/2/190/288) as follows:-

1816: 29th May: Stirling & Watt: Peter Stirling Gentleman's Servant of Jamaica Street No.23 and Helen Watt, daughter of John Watt Smith, of Water of Leith No.240 residing there, gave up their names for proclamation of Banns Matrimonial: James Watt Smith Rose Street No.83, Robert Hunter Wright Rose Street No.103

Peter and Helen had four known children in Edinburgh; Margaret (b. ~1822), John (b. ~1823), Peter (b. ~1826), and William (b. ~1828). In 1837 Pigot's Trade Directory, Peter Stirling was listed as a stable keeper at Rose Street Lane, St George's, Edinburgh. In 1841, Peter Stirling, 45, a horse dealer, resided at 118 Princes Street, St George's, Edinburgh, with wife Helen, 40, children Margaret, 20, John, 18, a journeyman stabler, Peter, 15, an apprentice saddler,

William, 13, a surgeon's apprentice, and Margaret Allan, 25, a female servant.

The tenement building at 118 Princes Street was part of the Edinburgh New Town constructions in the late 18th Century, although with later decorative additions to the façade in the late 19th-century. It is currently the site of the HSBC bank on Princes Street and it is a Grade B Listed Building. Peter, a horse dealer, was still alive in 1846.

Jimmy's maternal great-grandparents - Thomas Hearty and Janet Templeton

Jimmy's maternal great-grandfather Thomas Hearty (or Harty) and his great-grandmother Janet Templeton were born around 1805 in Ireland. Son William Hearty was born around 1833 in Ireland to father Thomas Hearty, a gardener, and mother Janet Templeton. Thomas and Janet were both dead by 1887.

Jimmy's paternal great-great-grandfather – John Watt

Jimmy's paternal great-great-grandfather John Watt was born around 1770 possibly in Edinburgh. John Watt, a blacksmith, had a daughter Helen (b. ~1797). John Watt, a blacksmith, at No.83 Rose Street, St George's, Edinburgh was still alive in 1816.

Chapter 11

James Hazeldean
Private 19241,
16th Battalion Royal Scots

James Hazeldean (1895 – 1980)

James William Hazeldean was born on 21 February 1895 at 4 Low Craigward, Alloa, Clackmannanshire, to father William Hazeldean, a bottle blower, and mother Betsy Mackie. His father William mistakenly registered his birthdate as 28 February, but this was amended in a Register of Corrected Entries signed by the Sheriff Substitute for Clackmannanshire. In 1901, James W, 6, a scholar, resided at Kelliebank, Alloa, with his father William Hazeldean, 29, a glass worker, mother Betsy, 25, and his two sisters. In 1911, James, 16, an apprentice bottle maker in Wood's Bottle Works, resided at 24 Ramsay Lane, Portobello, Edinburgh, with his father William Hazeldean, 39, a glass bottle blower, mother Betsy, 34, and his other siblings.

Jimmy was a professional footballer who played outside left for Heart of Midlothian, having previously played at Junior level. He was on Hearts books from 1915 to 1919, making five appearances in season 1915–16. On 1 July 1915, McCartney was assembling his squad for the coming season and had recruited two local Juniors, Jimmy Hazeldean and Teddy McGuire, both enlisted privates in the Heriot's reserve company of McCrae's Battalion. Hazeldean, 20, was a bottle blower in Wood's Bottle Works, like his father William before him, and, by then, living in Portobello.

Hazeldean had enlisted as a private in McCrae's Battalion and later served in the Labour Corps during the war. On 14 March 1916, McCrae's, having had its stint on the front-line at Bois Grenier, was relieved by the 27th Northumberland Fusiliers during a fierce German bombardment. They moved back for a well-earned break at Erquinghem. They were joined at Erquinghem by a replacement draft from Ripon, led by Lt. Harry Rawson. Among the 43 other ranks were Jimmy Hazeldean and Teddy McGuire.

Before the 7.30am whistle on 1 July 1916 to go over the top, Jimmy sat quietly with pals Duncan Currie and Harry Wattie. By late morning Jimmy was still attacking with Lionel Coles C Company, which had remained fairly intact in the sunken road below La Boisselle. During the murderous charge towards the village, Hazeldean was shot in the thigh on that dreadful first day on the Somme. The following day, as fighting continued, wounded stragglers started to return to the British lines from the direction of Contalmaison. Corporal Michael Kelly and Private Jimmy Hazeldean arrived together, holding each other up and stating, they were, "*one good man between the two of us.*"

Jimmy was transferred to a hospital in Middlesex, England where an 'explosive' round was removed from his leg. He never returned to the 'old 16th', which was scattered to the winds by the end of the Somme campaign, and after a short spell in the Labour Corps, he was discharged on medical grounds from the army. Private 19241 (382079

Labour Corps) James Hazeldean was awarded the Victory and British War medals.

After the war, Jimmy went back to his job as a bottle blower, by then the United Glass Bottle Works in Baileyfield Crescent, Portobello. He played in a friendly match for Hearts on 2 January 1919, but his footballing career was effectively over. Jimmy was one of the few who escaped the 'curse of the old 16th' and ended up living a long life. James William Hazeldean, 85, died in 1980 in Montrose, Angus.

Jimmy's parents -
William Hazeldean and Betsy Stewart Mackie

Jimmy's father William Hazeldean (various variants) was born on 7 July 1872 at Bannockburn, Stirlingshire to father James Hazeldean, a stone quarrier, and mother Margaret Annan. Bannockburn was the historic site of the famous battle on 23–24 June 1314 when Robert the Bruce, King of Scots, decisively defeated King Edward II of England, in the First War of Scottish Independence.

Jimmy's mother Betsy Stewart Mackie was born on 22 August 1876 in Brand's Row, Waterloo, Cambusnethan, Lanarkshire to father Robert Mackie, a coal miner, and mother Margaret Baxter. The mining village of Waterloo, also named after another historic battle, has a family history connection to two other more modern Hearts players, as recorded in Pride of the Bears, the third book in the Pride Series. Alfie Conn Senior, of Hearts famous 'Terrible Trio', and Alfie Conn Junior, who also controversially played for Rangers and Celtic, had ancestors who lived and worked in Waterloo, Cambusnethan.

In 1881, William, 8, a scholar, resided at 52 Drysdale Street, Alloa, with his father James Hazeldean, 50, a quarryman, mother Margaret, 45, and his other siblings. William met his sweetheart Betsy at the Alloa Glass Works on Craigward Street. The glass works was founded in 1750 and still operates today as United Glass. One of the original glass cones, of circa 1825, survives and houses one of the modern glass furnaces.

William Hazeldean, 22, a bottle-maker, married Betsy Mackie, 19, a bottle packer, both of Low Craigieward Place, Alloa, on 27 April 1894 in Alloa. The wedding was conducted by Rev George Mitchell, minister of St Andrew's Church of Scotland, Alloa; the best man was Allan Morton and the best maid was Maggie Elder. William and Betsy had seven known children; in Alloa, James William (b. 21 February 1895), Margaret, aka Maggie (b. ~1897), Hannah (b. ~1899), Robert (b. ~1902), John (b. ~1905); in Portobello, William (b. ~1907) and Betsy (b. ~1910). Son James William Hazeldean was born on 21 February 1895 at 4 Low Craigward, Alloa, Clackmannanshire, to father William Hazeldean, a bottle blower, and mother Betsy Mackie.

In 1901, William Hazeldean, 29, a glass worker, resided at Kelliebank, Alloa, with wife Betsy, 25, children James W, 6, a scholar, Maggie, 4, and Hannah, 2. Around 1906, William transferred his job to Wood's Bottle Works in Baileyfield Crescent, Portobello, Edinburgh. Wood's Bottle Works later became part of the United Glass Bottle Works. In 1911,

William Hazeldean, 39, a glass bottle blower, resided at 24 Ramsay Lane, Portobello, Edinburgh, with wife Betsy, 34, children James, 16, an apprentice bottle maker, Maggie, 14, recently left school, Hannah, 12, Robert, 9, John, 6, all scholars, William, 4, and Betsy, 2.

Jimmy's paternal grandparents - James Hazeldean and Margaret Annan

Jimmy's paternal grandfather James Hazeldean (various variants) was born around 1829 in Ovenden, Halifax, Yorkshire, England, to father Joseph Hazeldean, a quarryman, and mother Hannah Smith. His grandmother Margaret Annan was born on 22 September 1835 in Tulliallan, Clackmannanshire to father Edward Annan and mother Margaret Higgins. The birth is recorded in the OPRs for Tulliallan (Ref: 397/3/86) as follows:-

1835: Edward Annan & Margaret Higgen a Daughter born 22nd September 1835} Margaret

In 1841, James, 12, resided at Mixenden Green, Halifax, Yorkshire, with his father Joseph Heselden, 35, mother Hannah, 35, and his siblings. In 1851, James, 22, a stone delver, resided at Ovenden, Halifax, Yorkshire, with his father Joseph Hesselden, 47, a stone delver, mother Hannah, 45, and his siblings.

James Hazeldean, a stone quarrier, was stated as married to Margaret Annan on 11 May 1861 in New Sauchie, Clackmannanshire. James and Margaret had five known

THE PRIDE OF THE HEARTS

children; Hannah (b. ~1864, Sauchie), Edward (b. ~1869, Bannockburn), William (b. 7 July 1872, Bannockburn), Joseph (b. ~1877, Alloa) and Alexander (b. ~ 1880, Alloa). In 1881, James Hazeldean, 50, a quarryman, resided at 52 Drysdale Street, Alloa, with wife Margaret, 45, children Hannah, 17, a woollen millworker, Edward, 12, William, 8, both scholars, Joseph, 4, and Alexander, 1.

Within a few years, James fell victim to one of the accursed diseases afflicting the Victorian era, phthisis, now called tuberculosis, and in poverty-stricken circumstances he was removed to the poorhouse. James Hazeldean, only 54, a quarryman of Alloa, died on 31 March 1886 in the Stirling Combination Poorhouse of phthisis as certified by Dr Robert Moodie MD. Margaret Hazeldean nee Annan, 62, died on 2 March 1897 at 8 High Craigward, Alloa of congestion of the liver and dropsy as certified by Dr J Paul Low MB CM.

Jimmy's maternal grandparents – Robert Mackie and Margaret Baxter

Jimmy's maternal grandfather Robert Mackie and his grandmother Margaret Baxter were born around 1840 possibly in Stirlingshire. Robert Mackie, a coal miner, married Margaret Baxter on 27 March 1874 in Muiravonside, Stirlingshire. Daughter Betsy Stewart Mackie was born on 22 August 1876 in Brand's Row, Waterloo, Cambusnethan, Lanarkshire to father Robert Mackie, a coal miner, and mother

Margaret Baxter. Robert Mackie, a coal miner, was dead by 1894, although, his wife Margaret was still alive then.

Jimmy's paternal great-grandparents – Joseph Hesselden and Hannah Smith

Jimmy's paternal great-grandfather Joseph Hesselden (various variants) was born around 1804 and great-grandmother Hannah Smith was born around 1806, both in Ovendon, Yorkshire, England. The Old English surname Hesselden originates from various locations, meaning 'valley of the hazel', and the earliest recording is Heseldene in County Durham in 1050. Joseph Hesselden, a quarryman, married Hannah Smith around 1827 in Ovenden, Yorkshire and they had seven known children there; James (b. ~1829), Elizabeth (b. ~1834), Sarah (b. ~1837), Grace (b. ~1839), Harriet (b. ~1843), Mary (b. ~1846) and John (b. ~1848).

In 1841, Joseph Heselden, 35, resided at Mixenden Green, Halifax, Yorkshire, with wife Hannah, 35, children James, 12, Elizabeth, 7, Sarah, 4, and Grace, 2. In 1851, Joseph Hesselden, 47, a stone delver, resided at Ovenden, Halifax, Yorkshire, with wife Hannah, 45, children James, 22, a stone delver, Elizabeth, 17, Sarah, 14, Grace, 12, Harriet, 8, all four throstle spinners in a spinning mill, Mary, 5, and John, 3. Joseph, a quarryman, and Hannah were both dead by 1886.

Jimmy's paternal great-grandparents –
Edward Annan and Margaret Higgins

Jimmy's other paternal great-grandfather Edward Annan (or Hannan) and his great-grandmother Margaret Higgins (or Higgen) were both born around 1790 probably in Stirlingshire. Edward Annan married Margaret Higgins on 6 December 1814 in Airth, Stirlingshire. The marriage is recorded in the OPRs for Airth (Ref: 469/3/179) as follows:-

1814: December 6th: Annan & Higgins: Edward Annan and Margaret Higgins both in this Parish were married

Daughter Margaret Annan was born on 22 September 1835 in Tulliallan, Clackmannanshire to father Edward Annan and mother Margaret Higgins. Edward and Margaret were both dead by 1897.

Chapter 12

James Low
Corporal,
16th Battalion Royal Scots

James Low (1894 – 1960)

James Low was born on 9 March 1894 at Bridgend, Kilbirnie, Ayrshire, to father Malcolm Thomson Low, a manager at a fishing net factory, and mother Maggie Darroch. His family later moved to Elgin where he was educated at Elgin Academy. In 1901, James, 7, a scholar, resided at Moray Place, Elgin, with his father Malcolm T Low, 33, a net manufacturer, mother Maggie, 31, and his other siblings. In 1911, James, 17, at school, still resided at Moray Place, Elgin, with his father Malcolm T Low, 43, a net manufacturer and employer, Maggie, 41, and his other siblings.

He began his football career as an outside right at Highland League side Elgin City, where he picked up the nickname Jamie. In 1912, Low was a young agricultural undergraduate at Edinburgh University, where he was spotted playing for the university side by the Hearts scouts. John McCartney signed Low for Hearts in 1913 as he was building his new squad, which the manager felt destined to win the 1914–15 League championship. It was proudly reported in the Elgin Courant on 3 April 1914 that Low had been selected to play for Hearts. At the close of season 1913–14, Hearts finished 4th for the second year in a row; McCartney knew he almost had the side he wanted. It was all to be cruelly ripped out of Hearts hands by the outbreak of war.

Slowly at first, McCartney saw his squad eroded by enlistment. On 5 August 1914, two players signed up, including first-team regular George Sinclair, but McCartney remained upbeat and he promoted Low to the first team. On Wednesday 25 November 1914, under mounting pressure from politicians and the press, Low was one of the eleven Hearts players who signed up for McCrae's Battalion. By 18 June 1915, Low had been promoted to corporal and he was part of the Heart's contingent, along with 1,100 men of McCrae's 16th, who marched from their billets at Heriot's down the Mound to their departure train at Edinburgh Waverley heading for Ripon, Yorkshire.

However, quickly spotted as a university undergraduate, Low was commissioned in 1916 as a 2nd Lieutenant in the 6th Seaforth Highlanders. He was wounded in action on two occasions, including a bad head injury in 1917, which ended his war and threatened to end his footballing career.

After the war ended, McCartney wanted to rebuild the team that was his '*Musketeer Spirit of 1914*', but he became entangled in internal Hearts politics. The board was unwilling to sanction funds to return the unproven Annan Ness and Jamie Low. In Low's case, they opted to persevere for another year with the old warhorse Geordie Sinclair, also returned from the war, and Low was given a free transfer. When the 1919–20 season started, the Edinburgh Evening News observed that Hearts were most unlike themselves. Without even any thanks from the board for nine monumental years, a disconsolate John McCartney resigned on 17 October 1919.

Passed over by the Hearts board, Low initially returned to play for his old club Elgin City. As his injuries recovered and his play improved, he was signed in March 1920 by Rangers as a backup to the established Sandy Archibald. In October 1921, he was snapped up by Newcastle United and became a star of their great team of the 1920s, alongside the incomparable Hughie Gallagher. Low played for seven seasons at St James's Park and in 1924 he won the FA Cup with the Magpies. In 1930, he retired from football and returned to Elgin, taking over the running of the family fishing net-manufacturing business.

In 1942, during WW2, when Singapore was overrun by the invading forces of the Japanese Imperial Army, his only son, David, was posted missing serving with the Manchesters. Lieutenant 129560 David William Low, 2nd Battalion Manchester Regiment, 22, was killed in action on 22 February 1942, the son of James and Mary Sophia Low and husband of Jose Maurine Low. His body was never recovered and he is commemorated in the CWGC's Singapore Civil Hospital Grave Cemetery on Column 5. James Low, 65, a fishing net-manufacturer, died on 5 March 1960 at Arvid, 9 Moray Place, Elgin of a coronary thrombosis.

Jamie's parents –
Malcolm Thomson Low and Margaret Darroch

Jamie's father Malcolm Thomson Low was born on 8 June 1867 at Bridgend, Kilbirnie, Ayrshire to father John Low, a net manufacturer, and mother Margaret Houston. His mother Margaret Darroch (or Durroch) was born illegitimately on 30 November 1869 at Bridge Street, Kilbirnie to mother Agnes Darroch, a farmer's daughter. Margaret's birth was registered by her Aunt Annie Durroch. In 1871, Margaret, 1, resided at Bridge Street, Kilbirnie, with her mother Agnes, 18, at the home of her grandfather James Darroch, 44, a spirit merchant, and her grandmother Agnes, 43. Maggie was effectively raised by her grandparents James and Agnes Darroch.

In 1881, Maggie, 11, a scholar, resided at Bridge Street, Kilbirnie, with her grandfather James Darroch, 54, a carting and spirit dealer, and her grandmother Agnes, 53. In 1891, Malcolm, 23, a mechanic in the family net factory, resided in the substantial 12-windowed Bridgend House, Kilbirnie, with his widowed father John Low, 55, a net manufacturer and employer, and his siblings.

Malcolm Thomson Low, 24, a fishing net factory mechanic, of Bridgend House, Kilbirnie, married Maggie Darroch, 22, of Bridgend, Kilbirnie, on 17 February 1892. The wedding was conducted by Rev Henry Buchan, minister of the Church of Scotland; the best man was Robert Low, Malcom's brother, and the best maid was Jessie Darroch, Maggie's cousin.

Malcolm and Maggie had seven known children; in Kilbirnie, John (b. ~1893), James, aka Jamie (b. 9 March 1894, d. 5 March 1960); in Elgin, Margaret Houston, aka Maggie (b. ~1898, d. 19 May 1990), William Houston (b. ~1899), Robert (b. ~1903), Malcolm Thomson (b. ~1908, d. 27 September 1965) and Arthur Eric (b. 7 June 1913, d. 11 May 1944). Son

James Low was born on 9 March 1894 at Bridgend House, Kilbirnie.

At that time there was a thriving fishing net industry in Kilbirnie and Malcolm was the manager at his father John Low's factory, a competitor of the Stoneyholm Mill Net Factory of W & J Knox Ltd. W & J Knox was established in 1778 as a textile and net manufacturer and is still currently in production at Mill Road, Kilbirnie.

By the late 19th century, in the midst of a 'herring boom' in the north east of Scotland, Malcolm moved his family to Elgin to start up his own net manufacturing business. Herring was extensively fished in Scottish waters in the North Sea. Cured and pickled herring was a great delicacy in Northern Europe at that time, with most of the herring caught being for the export markets.

In 1901, Malcolm T Low, 33, a net manufacturer and employer, resided in upmarket Moray Place, Elgin, with wife Maggie, 31, children John, 8, James, 7, Maggie H, 3, all scholars, and William H, 2. In 1911, Malcolm T Low, 43, a net manufacturer and employer, still resided at Moray Place, Elgin, with wife Maggie, 41, children John, 18, a clerk in his father's net factory, James, 17, William H, 12, Robert, 8, all scholars, and Malcolm T, 3. In 1912, Malcolm and Margaret were proud to see their son Jamie leave Elgin Academy and enter Edinburgh University as an agricultural undergraduate. The following year Malcolm and Maggie had another son Arthur Eric born on 7 June 1913 at Moray Place, Elgin.

Malcolm Thomson Low, 74, a net manufacturer, died on 27 May 1941, during WW2, in Elgin. The following year his grandson Lt David W Low, 2nd Manchesters, was killed in action on 22 February 1942 in Singapore. In spring 1944, Allied forces tried to break through the German Gustav line on a 20 mile front from the western seaboard of Naples to Monte Cassino, sustaining heavy casualties. Further tragedy struck the Low family when youngest son Major 66574 Arthur Eric Low, MC and Bar, 6th Seaforth Highlanders, only 30, died of wounds in a military hospital in Naples on 11 May 1944. He served in the same battalion his older brother Jamie had in WW1 and is commemorated with honour in CWGC's Naples War Cemetery. A few weeks later the Gustav Line was finally breached and the US Army entered Rome on 4 June 1944.

Margaret Low nee Darroch, 82, died on 27 August 1951 of senility in a private nursing home in Lossiemouth, Morayshire.

Jamie's paternal grandparents – John Low and Margaret Houston

Jamie's paternal grandfather John Low was born around 1835 in Inveresk and Musselburgh, Edinburghshire (now Midlothian) to father John Low, a blacksmith, and mother Margaret Howard Henderbie. Jamie's grandmother Margaret Houston was born on 6 July 1838 at Bridgend, Kilbirnie to father James Houston, a weaver, and mother Jean Martin. The birth is recorded in the OPRs for the parish of Kilbirnie (Ref: 596/2/114) as follows:-

1838: July: [Born] 6: [Baptized] 15: Margaret Daughter Lawfull to James Houston Weaver at Bridge and Jean Martin

In 1841, John, 6, resided at Bridge Street, North Esk, Midlothian, with his widowed mother Mrs [Margaret] Low, 30, and his sister Helen, 9. In 1851, John Low, 15, a mechanic, lodged at Bridgend, Kilbirnie, where he met Margaret Houston in a local net factory and this began the long association with net manufacturing in the Low family. John Low, 20, a mechanic, married Margaret Houston, 17, a net weaver, both of Kilbirnie, on 28 August 1855. The wedding was conducted by Rev John Orr, minister of Kilbirnie Church of Scotland; the witness was Robert Knox.

John and Margaret had nine known children in Kilbirnie; William Houston (b. ~1858), John (b. ~1860), Robert (b. ~1865), Malcolm Thomson (b. 8 June 1867), Margaret, aka Maggie (b. ~1869), Jeanie (b. ~1872), Arthur (b. ~1874), Annie (b. ~1876) and Mary Ann (b. ~1883). In 1861, John Low, 26, an iron turner, resided at Bank Street, Kilbirnie, with wife Margaret, 23, sons William, 3, John, 10 months old, and their niece Amelia Houston, 9, a scholar.

However, John was ambitious and saw an opportunity to open his own net manufacturing factory in Kilbirnie. Son Malcolm Thomson Low was born on 8 June 1867 at Bridgend, Kilbirnie, to father John Low, a net manufacturer, and mother Margaret Houston. Margaret Low nee Houston, only 52, died on 5 December 1890 at Bridgend House, Kilbirnie of tetanus (known as lockjaw) as certified by James Milroy, surgeon.

Tetanus is an infection usually caused by the bacteria Clostridium tetani getting into an open wound. Unfortunately for Margaret, although a vaccine for tetanus was discovered by German scientist Emil von Behring in that same year of 1890, it was not until 1924 that a mass vaccination programme was introduced.

In 1891, John Low, 55, a net manufacturer and employer, still resided in the substantial 12-windowed Bridgend House, Kilbirnie, with his children Robert, 26, a net factory manager, Malcolm, 23, a mechanic in the net factory, Maggie, 22, Jeanie, 19, Arthur, 17, a clerk and cabinetmaker, Annie, 15, Mary A, 8, both scholars, and two servants Jeanie Kennedy, 26, a domestic cook, and Mary Robertson, 17, a general domestic servant. John Low married a second wife Marion Hogg in 1896 in Kilbirnie.

John Low, 75, a net manufacturer of Bridgend House, Kilbirnie, died on 10 March 1910. In his Will dated 1911 lodged at Kilmarnock Sheriff Court, John left Bridgend House to his son William Houston Low, a sum of £300 to his second wife Marion and the remainder of his estate of £691 19s 10d (approximately £54k currently) was divided between his other children. Years later, Houston Architects, possibly related to the Houston lineage, moved into Bridgend House, which was eventually demolished and the site is now the iconic 1930s Art Deco Radio City building.

Jamie's maternal grandmother –
Agnes Darroch (or Durroch)

Jamie's maternal grandmother Agnes Darroch (or Durroch) was born around 1853 in Kilbirnie, Ayrshire to father James Darroch, a farmer, and mother Agnes Mathie. In 1861, Agnes, 8, a scholar, resided at Bridgend Street, Kilbirnie, with her father James Darroch, 34, a farmer, mother Agnes, 33, and her other siblings. Aged only 16, Agnes fell pregnant and she gave birth to a girl. Daughter Margaret Darroch (or Durroch) was born illegitimately on 30 November 1869 at Bridge Street, Kilbirnie to mother Agnes Darroch, a farmer's daughter. Margaret's birth was registered by her Aunt Annie Durroch, as Agnes was too young to register her daughter.

In 1871, Agnes, 18, resided at Bridge Street, Kilbirnie, with her daughter Margaret, 1, her father James Darroch, 44, a spirit merchant, mother Agnes, 43, and her other siblings. Effectively, her daughter Margaret was raised by her grandparents and, in 1879, Agnes settled down to marriage. Agnes Darroch, 26, married Allan Walker, 25, a joiner journeyman, both of Bridge Street, Kilbirnie, on 28 March 1879. The wedding was conducted by Rev John Orr, minister of Church of Scotland; the best man was William Graham and the best maid was Jane Kerr. Agnes Walker nee Darroch was still alive in Kilbirnie in 1892.

Jamie's paternal great-grandparents –
John Low and Margaret Howard Henderby

Jamie's paternal great-grandfather John Low was born around 1805 probably in Inveresk and Musselburgh. His great-grandmother Margaret Howard Henderby (or Henderbie) was born around 1810 in Inveresk and Musselburgh to father Thomas Henderby, a corporal in the 73rd Regiment, and mother Anne Matthews. John and Margaret grew up in the busy fishing village of Fisherrow. There has been fishing at Fisherrow and Musselburgh since Roman times, and the present 17th-century harbour is very close to the Roman harbour at the mouth of the River Esk that served the Inveresk Roman Fort on the high ground east of the Esk upriver. The Fisherrow fishermen used to fish for herring and later for whitefish.

John Low, a blacksmith, married Margaret Howard Henderbie, both of Fisherrow, Musselburgh, on 7 December 1827. The marriage is recorded in the OPRs for the parish of Inveresk and Musselburgh (Ref: 689/18/168) as follows:-

1827: Low John, blacksmith, residing in Fisherrow & Margaret Howard Hendribie [sic], daughter of the late Thomas Hendribie, also residing in Fisherrow, gave in their names for proclamation of banns on the 7th December 1827. Cautioner for the man John Gibson & for the woman Thomas Low

John and Margaret had two known children; daughter Helen (b. ~1832) and son John (b. ~1835) in Inveresk and Musselburgh, Edinburghshire. John Low, a blacksmith, was probably dead by 1837, as he is not listed in Pigot's Trade Directory of 1837, although, his best man John Gibson is listed as a blacksmith at New Street, Fisherrow. In 1841, Mrs [Margaret] Low, 30, a widow, resided at Bridge Street, North Esk, with daughter Helen, 9, and son John, 6. It is likely that

Margaret Howard Low nee Henderbie was dead by 1851. At that time her daughter Helen, 19, was a house servant for Mrs Elizabeth Thomson at High Street, Musselburgh and her son John, 15, worked as a factory mechanic at Bridgend, Kilbirnie.

Jamie's paternal great-grandparents – James Houston and Jane Martin

Jamie's other paternal great-grandfather James Houston and his great-grandmother Jane Martin, aka Jean, were probably born around 1810 in Kilbirnie, Ayrshire. James Houston, a weaver, married Jean Martin and they had a known daughter Margaret (b. 6 July 1838) at Bridgend, Kilbirnie. James, a weaver, and Jean were still alive in 1855 in Kilbirnie.

Jamie's maternal great-grandparents – James Darroch and Agnes Mathie

Jamie's maternal great-grandfather James Darroch (or Durroch), aka Jimmie, was born around 1827 in Kilbirnie, Ayrshire. His great-grandmother Agnes Mathie was born around 1828 in Houston, Renfrewshire. James Darroch, a farmer, married Agnes Mathie and they had ten known children in Kilbirnie; Alexander (b. ~1848), Agnes (b. ~1853), Andrew (b. ~1855), Jane (b. ~1857), James (b. ~1860), John (b. ~1862), Robert (b. ~1864), Elizabeth (b. ~1867), Mary (b. ~1870) and Jessie (b. ~1873). In 1861, James Darroch, 34, a farmer of 50 acres, resided at Bridgend Street, Kilbirnie, with wife Agnes, 33, children Alexander, 13, Agnes, 8, a scholar, Andrew, 5, Jean, 3, James, 1, and a domestic servant Elizabeth Allison, 20.

James was still working as a farmer in 1869, however, by 1871 he was trading as a spirit merchant. In 1871, James Darroch, 44, a spirit merchant, resided at Bridge Street, Kilbirnie, with wife Agnes, 43, children Alexander, 22, a farm labourer, Agnes, 18, Andrew, 16, a clerk, Jane, 14, at home, James, 11, John, 9, Robert, 7, all scholars, Elizabeth, 4, Mary, 8 months old, and granddaughter Margaret, 1. In 1881, James Darroch, 54, a carting and spirit merchant, still resided at Bridge Street, Kilbirnie, with wife Agnes, 53, children John, 19, a commercial clerk, Elizabeth, 14, household duties, Mary, 10, Jessie, 8, both scholars, granddaughter Maggie, 11, a scholar, and servant Thomas Lowrie, 26, a carter. 'Jimmie Darroch's Pub' became part of Kilbirnie folklore as recorded in Kilbirnie Heritage by Robert Houston.

'Old Darroch's' was the favourite howff of the local worthies and the upstairs dance hall was used for wedding receptions. During the turn of the 20th century it was found necessary to widen the stone bridge over the Garnock, and so the pub, John Thomson's smiddy

Jamie's paternal great-great-grandparents – Thomas Henderby and Anne Mathews

Jamie's paternal great-great-grandfather Thomas Henderby (or Henderbie) was born around 1785 possibly in Lincoln, Lincolnshire, England. His great-great-grandmother Anne Mathews was born around 1784 possibly in Inveresk and Musselburgh. Thomas Henderby enlisted in the Aberdeenshire Militia and by 1807 he was transferred to the 73rd (Perthshire) Regiment of Foot and during the Napoleonic Wars he was a Corporal stationed in Midlothian. Thomas Henderby, a Corporal in the 73rd Regiment, married Anne Mathews on 1 August 1807 in Inveresk. The marriage is recorded in the OPRs for the parish of Inveresk and Musselburgh (Ref: 689/13/202) as follows:-

1807: Henderby Thomas, Corporal in the 73rd Regiment, & Anne Mathews both in this parish gave in their names for proclamation of Marriage on the 1 August 1807. Cautioner for the man Charles George Gray & for the woman Robert Mathews

Thomas and Anne had two known children; Margaret Howard Henderby (b. ~1810) and a son Thomas Henderby (b. ~1820) in Inveresk and Musselburgh.

Thomas's best man Charles George Gray was born on 28 November 1786 in Edinburgh, son of Colonel Gray of the 75th Regiment. It is likely that Charles Gray and Thomas Henderby served together in India as both regiments were present at the siege of Bhurtpore in 1804. Gray later rose to the rank of Lieutenant Colonel and in 1814 his regiment was ordered to reinforce New Orleans, but was held up in Cork, Ireland by unfavourable winds. Signals were received that Napoleon Bonaparte had escaped from Elba and Gray's regiment was diverted to Flanders, where he fought with distinction at Quatre Bras and Waterloo in 1815.

The 73rd Regiment also fought at Quatre Bras and Waterloo, repelling eleven French cavalry charges, and it is almost certain Corporal Thomas Henderby fought during the two decisive battles concluding the Napoleonic Wars. Thomas would not know his descendant James Low would also fight on Flanders Field a century later. The 73rd Regiment, which later became the famous Black Watch, spent two years in Paris as part of the Allied Occupation of France and Thomas was discharged in 1817 when the regiment was disbanded.

Thomas Henderby became a Chelsea Pensioner and worked as a barber in Musselburgh. Thomas Henderby, 43, a barber, died on 7 March 1820 as recorded in the OPRs for the parish of Inveresk and Musselburgh (Ref: 689/15/242) as follows:-

1820: March: Henderby: Thomas Henderby Barbar [sic] in Musselburgh died upon the 7 and was Burried upon the 10 about nine feet east of the Session House ~ aged 43 years

In 1841, son John Henderby, 20, an apprentice flesher, resided at Liberton Park, Midlothian, the residence of James Stewart, 40, a farmer and flesher. In the Ordnance Survey of 1852 Liberton Park was described as 'an old house three storeys high in good repair'. John Henderby later became a master butcher residing at 2 Monteith Row, Calton, Glasgow.

Ann Henderby nee Mathews, known as Ann Tait, 74, widow of a Chelsea Pensioner, died at Fisherrow, Musselburgh in 1858.

Chapter 13

Edward McGuire
Private 12190,
16th Battalion Royal Scots

Edward McGuire (1893 – 1941)

Edward McGuire was born on 12 August 1893 at Whiterigg, Airdrie, Lanarkshire, to father Edward McGuire, a coal miner, and mother Catherine Whelan. The birth was registered by his father Edward, who signed with his 'x' mark, on 18 August 1893 at the Airdrie Registry Office. Edward, sponsored by Mrs Finlay, was baptized on 16 August 1893 by Fr Hugh J Kidd at St Margaret's RC Church, Airdrie. Known as Teddy, he started out in the amateur ranks playing for local miners' sides Kenmuirhill Athletic, then Shettleston and Parkhead Juniors. Considering McGuire's footballing transfers heading towards the east end of Glasgow and his fiercely proud Irish heritage, it is likely that he had hopes of playing for Celtic. He was almost certainly scouted, but never seriously considered by Willie Maley, the legendary Celtic manager.

While working as a coal miner, he played for the Central League club Armadale FC. Armadale had formed as a senior club in March 1910 and they lost 2–0 in their opening friendly against Rangers, with McGuire trialling in the game in the forward line at inside-right. In 1911, Edward McGuire,

17, a coal miner hewer, boarded at a widowed housekeeper Lizzie McGowan's home in the village of Mount Vernon, Boghall and Broomhouse, in the quoad sacra parish of Kenmuir. McGuire was a miner at Kenmuirhill Colliery and played for the miners' team Kenmuirhill Athletic in season 1911–12. In 1912 he moved to Shettleston Juniors and the following year he played for Parkhead Juniors in 1913–14.

Six days after Britain declared war on Germany, McGuire signed professionally for Armadale on 10 August 1914. Senior football played on despite growing criticism in some quarters. On 14 August 1914 the West Lothian Courier reported that McGuire had appeared in a pre-season friendly.

In the second half the Blue team secured more of the game, and Christie got a nice goal. On the other hand, McGuire and Davidson, of the opposing lot, each got one. A very interesting game finished – White team, 4 goals; Blue team, 1 goal.

On 14 September 1914, the Courier reported McGuire playing in a local derby game against Bathgate.

Ryan, fouling close in, gave Armadale a chance. A scrimmage ensued, and McGuire drove a low fast ball, but it went wide of its billet.

On 1 January 1915, the Courier reported a game between Alloa and Armadale.

"Then a corner was secured, which McGuire placed beautiful, and Bain shot in."

On 22 January 1915, in a game against Forfar under the headline:

Armadale Keep Forging Ahead - *For a few minutes Armadale were in queer street, but Whyte got away, and after a big forward dash, McGuire with a swift low shot, beat Scott all the way.*

At that time, Armadale, were on a successful run, winning the Central League titles in 1913–14 and 1914–15, although they eventually ran into financial difficulties and went defunct in 1932. On 30 April 1915, Armadale secured the league title against Arbroath under the headline "Armadale's Splendid Finish" with McGuire playing at inside right.

McGuire's impressive season had brought him to the attention of the Hearts manager. On 7 May 1915, the *Courier* reported:

This week McCartney of the Hearts paid a visit to Armadale. He had a confab with Williamson and McGuire. Williamson also received the attention of Brannigan of the Hibs and W. Maley, Celtic. So far there is nothing doing, however, for Williamson and McGuire are not too anxious to commit themselves meantime. They have a chance, too, for honours in the Emerald Isle.

McGuire finally made up his mind and was signed as an inside-right for Hearts on 1 July 1915 by McCartney to bolster his rapidly diminishing squad. In August 1915 the Edinburgh Evening News reported that McGuire had signed for Hearts as a clever, bustling player, although he lacked some height. It was also reported that he had recently had a trial for Arsenal.

In the Hearts minutes for 31 August 1915, Armadale FC pressed Hearts for the £10 transfer fee in lieu of '*E. McGuire*'. Due to the financial strictures brought about by war, Hearts offered Armadale a benefit match in lieu of payment, although the minute suggested, as McGuire had already enlisted, this effectively reverted him to amateur status. At the recording of the minute, Teddy was enlisted as a Private in the Heriot's reserve company of the Royal Scots. Teddy made three appearances for Hearts between 14 August 1915 and 3 January 1916, scoring one goal.

By 14 March 1916, Teddy McGuire and Jimmy Hazeldean, led by Lieutenant Harry Rawson, had settled into the 16th Divisional reserve camp at Erquinghem. On that bright blue, breathless summer morning of 1 July 1916, just after 6.30am, the British shelling of the German trenches in front of La Boisselle intensified. Teddy McGuire and Alfie Briggs sat quietly on the fire-step writing letters home, passing them to CQMS Donald Gunn for safe-keeping. At 7.30am as the whistles blew, Captain Lionel Coles, his shirt sleeves rolled up to the elbow, led C Company over the parapet into No Man's Land. By some miracle, C Company made it reasonably intact and were hunkered down in the sunken road below the village of La Boisselle.

Coles ordered a further charge up the road and the company ran straight into a nest of German machine-guns. In the carnage that ensued McGuire was badly injured. In a letter back to McCartney, it was reported:

Teddy McGuire was struck in the arm by flying shrapnel. As he fell, a machine gun round grazed his head.

He was shipped back to Britain and ended up in Stobhill Hospital in Glasgow, where he slowly recuperated from his wounds. McGuire was transferred to the 18th (Reserve) Training Battalion Royal Scots, which had been based in Dundee since 1916. His arm never fully recovered and he was eventually invalided out of the army. Private 12190 Edward McGuire, Royal Scots was awarded the Victory and British War Medals. Although he remained on Hearts books until 1918, he never played for the Gorgie side again.

On 22 June 1918, Belfast United signed McGuire from Hearts and he then transferred to another Belfast club Distillery. McGuire had arrived in Ireland at a period of political upheaval, which had been brewing since the Easter Rising in Dublin in 1916. After major gains in December 1918, Sinn Fein won a landslide victory and on 21 January 1919 they formed the Dáil Éireann, declaring an independent Ireland. This sparked the Irish War of Independence (1919–21), eventually leading to the formation of the Irish Free State. McGuire's politics are unknown, but given that he was born in Scotland, but chose to play for the national Irish League side, states where his heart lay.

In November 1920, McGuire had a two-week trial period with Preston North End. On 11 November 1920, the Lancashire Evening Post reported McGuire's trial:

If his papers come through in time, Edward McGuire, a new inside forward, will make his debut in the reserve

*team in the return game against Stockport County Res.
McGuire, who comes from the Belfast Distillery Club,
was chosen to play for the Irish League in the Inter-
league match with Scotland, at Glasgow the other
week, when, however, fog prevented a start.*

On 18 November 1920, the Evening Post reported:

*"North End Reserve will meet Bury Reserve at Deepdale
with a team which is expected to include Edward
McGuire, the inside forward from Belfast Distillery."
The next day, the paper reported, "North End Reserve
have made important changes for the match with Bury
Reserve, at Deepdale...which will probably include
Edward McGuire, the Belfast Distillery forward. The
doubt concerning this new player's appearance is due
to the dilatoriness of the Irish authorities in dealing
with his papers." McGuire returned to Belfast
disappointed.*

In January 1921, Bathgate signed the former Armadale
and Hearts man, still on Belfast Distillery's books. In August
1921, he signed for Abertillery Town in the Welsh National
League. At some point he returned to Northern Ireland
where he married his wife Mary Connor around 1923, and
was established with Newtonards side Ards FC by March
1926. On 20 March 1926, Ards player McGuire played for the
Irish League against the League of Ireland.

On 17 May 1926 McGuire played a game for Shamrock
Rovers, which was in breach of professional rules. He was
suspended for twelve months by the Irish FA for signing for
Shamrock Rovers before his agreement with Ards had

expired. The *Athletic News* reported on 2 August 1926 that '*E. McGuire, the inside-right of Ards*', was already heading for Philadelphia, USA.

It appears that McGuire initially sailed to Canada, possibly seeking a footballing contract in one of the North American leagues. He disembarked from the SS Montrose on 6 August 1926 at Quebec heading for 320 Magdalen Street, Montreal, giving his birthplace as '*Airdrey,(sic) Scotland*', but his nationality as Scotch-Irish. His wife Mary was still living in Belfast and it appears he returned briefly to Northern Ireland.

On 12 August 1927, eight professional footballers from Northern Ireland sailed from Liverpool to Montreal, including Edward McGuire, 34, although, it seems his professional football career was over by 1930. In 1930 US census, Edward McGuire, 36, from Scotland, resided in The Bronx, New York with wife Mary C McGuire, 26, from Ireland. McGuire was working as a labourer at the Edison Plant, founded by Thomas Edison (1847–1931), the inventor and philanthropist. Like many of the other Hearts players, it appears that Edward McGuire fell to the 'curse of the old 16th' and he died, aged just 47, in New York in 1941.

Teddy's parents –
Edward McGuire and Catherine Whelan

Teddy's father Edward McGuire was born on 29 December 1861 at 18 East Row, Ballochney, New Monkland, Lanarkshire, to father John McGuire, a collier, and mother

Bridget Costello. His mother Catherine Whelan (or Wheelan or Whilan) was born around 1863 at Whiterigg, New Monkland, Lanarkshire to father Patrick Whelan, a labourer, and mother Julia Bamrick. In 1871, Catherine, 8, a scholar, resided at Whiterigg, Clarkston, New Monkland, with her father Patrick Whelan, 37, a labourer, mother Julia, 32, and her siblings.

Edward McGuire, 21, a coal miner, married Catherine Whelan, 18, an outdoor worker, who signed with her 'x' mark', both of South Stanrigg, New Monkland, on 2 December 1883 at St Margaret's RC Church, Airdrie. The wedding was conducted by Fr James McIntosh, RC clergyman; the best man was James Kelly and the best maid was Margaret Whelan, Catherine's sister. Edward and Catherine had nine known children in Airdrie; John (b. ~1885), Julia (b. ~1887), Bridget (b. ~1889), Catherine (b. ~1891), Edward (b. 12 August 1893), Mary Ann (b. ~1896), Margaret, aka Maggie (b. ~1900), Helen, aka Nellie (b. ~1902) and Patrick (b. ~1903).

In 1891, Edward McGuire, 28, an ironstone miner, resided at 11 Whiterigg Row, Whiterigg, Clarkston by Airdrie, with wife Catherine, 25, children John, 6, a scholar, Julia, 4, Bridget, 2, and Catherine, 2 months old. The Whiterigg Coal Pit was opened in 1829 by Robert Miller and Robert Addie, owners of the Dundyvan Iron Works, and from 1830 it was served by the Whiterigg, Stanrigg, Arbuckle and Arden Branch of the Ballochney Railway Company. The line was closed before 1890.

Son Edward McGuire, aka Teddy, was born on 12 August 1893 at Whiterigg, Airdrie, Lanarkshire, to father Edward McGuire, a coal miner, and mother Catherine Whelan. The birth was registered by his father Edward, who signed with his 'x' mark, on 18 August 1893 at the Airdrie Registry Office.

In 1911, Edward McGuire, 48, a coal miner hewer, resided at Stanrigg Cottage, Whiterigg, Airdrie, with wife Catherine, 46, children Julia, 24, a cotton mill worker, Mary Ann, 15, and Maggie, 11, Nellie, 9, Patrick, 8, all three at school. Also boarding at Edward's home was brother-in-law James Whelan, 42, a coal miner hewer, and visiting was Mary Ann McGuire, only 1 month old.

Edward McGuire, 65, a coal miner, of Station Row, Whiterigg by Airdrie, died on 9 June 1928 in the Royal Infirmary, Townhead, Glasgow, of a fractured skull as certified by Dr Isabel B Wiese MB ChB. The death was registered by Edward's son Patrick McGuire, of Station Row, Whiterigg, on 11 June 1928 at the Glasgow Registry Office. In a Register of Corrected Entries, Edward McGuire, 65, was recorded with a cause of death by '*a fractured skull the result of being knocked down by a motorcycle*' as certified by Robert J Waugh, Procurator Fiscal, dated 19 June 1928 at Airdrie. At that time, his son Teddy had immigrated to New York City.

Catherine McGuire nee Whelan, 86, widow of Edward McGuire, coal miner, died on 20 December 1949 at 114 Jarvie Avenue, Plains by Airdrie of acute cardiac failure, myocarditis and arteriosclerosis as certified by Dr John H Kennedy LRCP&S Edin. The death was registered by her daughter Mary Ann McGuire on 21 December 1949 at the Airdrie Registry Office.

Teddy's paternal grandparents –
John McGuire and Bridget Costello

Teddy's paternal grandfather John McGuire was born around 1833 in Ireland to father Edward McGuire, a hawker of small wares, and mother Mary McGuire. His grandmother Bridget Costello (or Costelly or Costlow), aka Bethia, was born around 1842 in Ireland to father Thomas Costello, a quarrier, and mother Margaret Welsh. John McGuire, 28, a coal miner, married Bridget Costello, 19, who signed with her 'x' mark, both of Ballochney, New Monkland on 16 January 1861 at St Margaret's RC Church, Airdrie. The wedding was conducted by Fr Duncan McNab, Catholic clergyman; the best man was John Hacket and the best maid was Eliza Hackney. John and Bridget had two known children in Ballochney; Mary (b. ~1860) and Edward (b. 29 December 1861).

In 1861, John McGuire, 28, an ironstone miner, resided at 18 East Row, Ballochney, with wife stated as Bethia, 19, and daughter Mary, under 9 months old. John's father Edward McGuire, 64, a hawker of small wares, and mother Mary, 66, resided two doors away at 16 East Row, Ballochney. Son Edward McGuire was born on 29 December 1861 at 18 East Row, Ballochney, New Monkland, to father John McGuire, a collier, and mother Bridget Costello. The birth was registered by Ann Costelly, who signed with her 'x' mark, possibly Bridget's sister, on 4 January 1862 at the New Monkland Registry Office. John McGuire, a coal miner, was deceased by 1883, although, his wife Bridget was still alive.

Teddy's maternal grandparents –
Patrick Whelan and Julia Bamrick

Teddy's maternal grandfather Patrick Whelan (or Wheelan or Whilan) was born around 1834 in Ireland to father Robert Whelan, a collier, and mother Catherine Toban. His maternal grandmother Julia Bamrick (or Balmrick or Bambrick) was born around 1836 in Ireland to father Martin Bamrick, a collier, and mother Mary Lauder. Patrick Whelan, 22, a collier, who signed with his 'x' mark, married Julia Bamrick, 20, both of Whiterigg, New Monkland, on 26 September 1856 at Airdrie. The wedding was conducted by Fr Duncan McNab, Catholic clergyman of St Margaret's RC Church, Airdrie; the best man was John Bamrick, who signed with his 'x' mark, and the best maid was Elizabeth Bamrick, who signed with her 'x' mark, probably Julia's brother and sister.

Patrick and Julia had seven known children in Whiterigg, New Monkland; Robert (b. ~1857), John (b. ~1859), Mary (b. ~1861), Catherine (b. ~1863), Margaret (b. ~1865), James (b. ~1868) and Julia (b. ~1870). Daughter Catherine Whelan was born around 1863 at Whiterigg, New Monkland, Lanarkshire to father Patrick Whelan, a labourer, and mother Julia Bamrick.

In 1871, Patrick Whelan, 37, a labourer, resided at Whiterigg, Clarkston, New Monkland, with wife Julia, 32, children Robert, 14, a labourer, John, 12, Mary, 10, Catherine, 8, all three scholars, Margaret, 6, James, 3, and Julia, 1. Patrick Whelan, a coal miner, and wife Julia were both still alive at Whiterigg in 1883.

Teddy's paternal great-grandparents –
Edward McGuire and Mary McGuire

Teddy's paternal great-grandfather Edward McGuire was born around 1797 in Ireland. His great-grandmother Mary McGuire (her married name) was born around 1795 in Ireland. Edward and Mary had a son John (b. ~1833). It is likely that the McGuire family emigrated to New Monkland, Lanarkshire in the period following the devastating Irish Potato Famine (1846–52). It is estimated that around 1 million Irish peasants perished through starvation and deprivation and that a million and a half Irish emigrated to Britain, North America and Australia. In 1861, Edward McGuire, 64, a hawker of small wares, resided at 16 East Row, Ballochney, with wife Mary, 66. Two doors away at 18 East Row, their son John McGuire, 28, an ironstone miner, lived with their daughter-in-law Bethia (Bridget), 19, and granddaughter Mary, under 9 months old.

Teddy's paternal great-grandparents –
Thomas Costello and Margaret Welsh

Teddy's other paternal great-grandfather Thomas Costello (or Costelly or Costlow) and great-grandmother Margaret Welsh (or Walshe) were born around 1810 in Ireland. Thomas and Margaret had two known daughters in Ireland; Bridget, aka Bethia, (b. ~1842) and Ann. Thomas Costello, a quarrier, was deceased by 1861, although, his wife Margaret was still alive then.

Teddy's maternal great-grandparents –
Robert Whelan and Catherine Toban

Teddy's maternal great-grandfather Robert Whelan and great-grandmother Catherine Toban were born around 1805 in Ireland. Robert Whelan, a collier, married Catherine Toban and they had a son Patrick (b. ~1834) in Ireland. Robert Whelan, a collier, and wife Catherine were still alive in 1856, probably in New Monkland.

Teddy's maternal great-grandparents –
Martin Bamrick and Mary Lauder

Teddy's other maternal great-grandfather Martin Bamrick and great-grandmother Mary Lauder were born around 1805 in Ireland. Martin Bamrick, a collier, married Mary Lauder and they had 3 known children in Ireland; Julia (b. ~1836), John and Elizabeth. Martin Bamrick, a collier, and wife Mary were still alive in 1856, probably in New Monkland.

Chapter 14

Annan Ness
Regimental Sergeant Major,
16th Battalion Royal Scots

Annan Ness (1892 – 1942)

Annan Buchan Ness was born on 5 May 1892 at 37 Victoria Road, Kirkcaldy, Fife, to father William Ness, a floor-cloth worker in a linoleum factory, and mother Catherine Ramsay Blyth. After leaving school, Ness initially worked in the Fife coalfields. When he was 19, Ness enlisted in the Royal Army Medical Corps from July 1911 to October 1913. Ness signed from junior team Bonnyrigg Rose Athletic for Hearts in August 1913, turning professional in October when he left the RAMC. He remained on the Tynecastle side's books until 1918. Two weeks into the war, the pressure was growing politically on professional footballers to enlist for King and country.

On 20 August 1914, manager McCartney announced that the entire playing staff would engage in weekly drill sessions to prepare them for possible military service. The drills were conducted at Grindlay Street Hall by second-team half-back, Annan Ness, having previously served in the RAMC. After an invitation from Hearts, several Hibernian players also joined the drills. Ness only made three first team appearances for Hearts in that fateful year, the first on New

Year's Day 1914 and his last on Christmas Day 1914. It was widely reported that British and German soldiers downed arms that same day and organised an unofficial international football match in No Man's Land.

Ness, still a second-team player, was part of the contingent of Hearts players who enlisted on 25 November 1914 and McCrae promoted the ex-soldier to Company Sergeant. Ness turned down McCrae's offer of a commission in order to remain with his pals in the ranks. On 26 February 1915, Sergeant Annan Ness was the best man at teammate Jimmy Frew's wedding to Jeanie Campbell. The following day an exhausted Hearts drew 2–2 at Easter Road, while Celtic beat Partick Thistle 2–0 at Firhill.

Hearts still had a slender one-point lead, but football training during the days followed by military drill in the evenings had completely worn the squad down. On 24 April, Celtic drew 1–1 with Motherwell to wrest the League championship from Hearts grasp. Criticism followed in the *Edinburgh Evening News*, directed at both Celtic and Rangers, for not sending a single prominent player to the army. *"There is only one football champion in Scotland, and its colours are maroon and khaki."* By the end of the season, Ness was promoted to Company Sergeant Major of Captain Lionel Coles' C Company.

After the 16th returned from their first actions in the line at Bois Grenier, the battalion was billeted at their reserve camp at Erquinghem. On 19 March 1916, Ness wrote to McCartney and informed him that Lieutenant Harry Rawson, Jimmy Hazeldean, and Teddy McGuire had joined the company, and also to give the manager a list of items required in a *'bumper comforts parcel'*. The huge parcel arrived on 31 March, including a melodeon for Paddy Crossan, ironically stamped *'Made in Germany'*.

On the fateful morning of 1 July 1916, Annan Ness and Jimmy Boyd were stationed at Coles' C Company HQ. The first day had been a disaster in terms of casualties, but the 15th and 16th had held the line at Wood Alley and Scots Redoubt. At 7.50am on 2 July, German bombing parties attacked Wood Alley at the British barricade at Horseshoe sap. German riflemen followed up the charge and a desperate exchange ensued against the Royal Scots. At the last moment, CSM Ness arrived with a bayonet section and repulsed the Germans. Colonel Sir George McCrae stood on the parapet at Scots Redoubt and *'dropped a Fritz with every shot'*.

The Germans retreated to lick their wounds and at 2.15am on 3 July bombing parties again assaulted the Scots Redoubt, followed ten minutes later by a full company attacking the centre of Wood Alley. They succeeded in entering the trench, but again they were met by Ness and a rifle section. After a bloody and brief encounter, the Germans again retreated. The 16th was relieved by units of the 23rd Division on the evening of 3 July. McCrae was the last man back to the British line and the stand at Scots Redoubt became part of British military folklore.

Sir George was awarded the DSO and the battalion received two Military Crosses and four Military Medals, but the toll of dead and injured during the opening days of the Somme was grievous. The Hearts pals were scattered to the four winds and refitting the battalion was underway. McCrae was never the same man again.

On 20 July, Ness wrote to McCartney: "*We had a match the other evening, but oh, Mr McC., we did miss the boys. Talk about football. It made the tears come to our eyes.*" As the Somme rumbled on throughout the summer of 1916, the 16th were set to go back into the line on 26 August, the objective being Cologne Ridge to open a frontal attack on the Hindenburg line. Although the Germans were pushed back towards Bellicourt, the battalion suffered more terrible losses by 28 August, when they were relieved.

On 11 September the 16th were back at Cologne Ridge. Ness had been promoted to Regimental Sergeant Major and five days later he received a note from John McCartney to say that Ernie Ellis's remains had been found. On the night of 22 October, McCrae's were in action at Poelcappelle, on the Passchendaele Ridge, coming under intense bombardment and strafing. Ness and a small band of men held the line, being relieved on the following morning.

Field Marshal Haig almost made the breakthrough on the Hindenburg line with a surprise tank attack at Cambrai on 20 November, but by 30 November the Germans had regained their losses and the killing season of the Somme came to an end. It is estimated that the Battle of the Somme saw half a million casualties sustained on both sides.

By 7 April 1918, McCrae's were back at Divisional reserve in Erquinghem in preparation for the final push. Around 8.30pm the Germans opened up a huge bombardment of shells and gas around Armentieres and heavy casualties ensued. The Germans then launched their final counter-attack to break through to the Flanders coast, with heavy fighting around Erquinghem. The 16th fought hard to hold the line. Lt Harry Rawson was shot in the throat and later died of his wound. By late afternoon the Germans were in Steenwerck and they had already taken Messines and Ploegsteert. The 16th were ordered to evacuate and the bridge at Erquinghem was blown up. RSM Ness remained in charge of the bridgehead until the early evening until he withdrew his command. The south bank of the River Lys fell to the Germans on 11 April.

On 16 May 1918, the 16th Royal Scots was disbanded, along with the heavily depleted 34th Division, and McCrae's Battalion was no more. RSM Ness was awarded the rare honour of a direct commission in the field as Lieutenant in the Royal Scots (Lothian Regiment). The Americans were now in Flanders and the 'Advance to Victory' began in August 1918.

Following the Armistice, the demobilised Ness returned to Hearts in 1919, but the new board refused to sanction McCartney the funds for the unproven Ness and he was released along with Jamie Low. Ness retired from football and trained to become a dental surgeon, however, he fell to the 'curse of the old 16th'. Although he had been living and practising dentistry in Beverley House at 132 High Street, Chesham, Buckinghamshire, he returned a dying man to his beloved Edinburgh. Beverley House, a red brick 2-storey terrace is a Grade II Listed Building by Historic England.

Annan Buchan Ness, only 50, died of cancer and a pulmonary embolism in a nursing home at 39 Palmerston Place, Edinburgh on 15 December 1942, during WW2, as certified by Dr J P Leckie MB. His death was registered by his widow Elizabeth Ann Ness nee Hillock. The 3-storey terrace including 39 Palmerston Place is a Category B Listed Building built by Alexander White and completed in 1884.

Annan's parents -
William Ness and Catherine Ramsay Blyth

Annan's father William Ness was born on 27 December 1859 at Sinclairtown, Dysart, Fife, to father David Ness, a linen weaver, and mother Jane Forrester. His mother Catherine Ramsay Blyth was born on 19 February 1864 at Harbour Head, Kirkcaldy, Fife, to father John Blyth, an iron moulder, and mother Janet Fyfe.

In 1861, Englishman Frederick Walton invented a new, durable and inexpensive floor-cloth covering, which he patented as linoleum. After the patent ran out in 1864, the Kirkcaldy firm of Michael Nairn & Co began mass-producing linoleum, in spite of a failed court action by Walton. Other firms also began in Kirkcaldy, such as Barry, Ostlere & Shepherd and this gave the town the moniker of 'Kirkcaldy – the linoleum capital of the world'. At its peak, Nairn's had seven factories over 55 acres and employed 4,000 workers.

Val McDermid, the Scottish crime writer, who was born in Kirkcaldy, recalls the effect the industry had on the town in a BBC Scotland documentary 'The Town That Floored the World'. She commented, "I think linoleum was at the heart of the town, because the factories were right at the heart of the town."

In 1871, William, 11, a scholar, resided at North Side High Street, Linktown, Kirkcaldy, with his father David Ness, 43, an unemployed linen weaver, mother Jane, 39, a millworker, and his three sisters. William Ness, 21, a floor-cloth worker in a linoleum factory, residing at Quality Street, Newton, Kirkcaldy, married Catherine R Blyth, 17, a power loom weaver in a linen factory, residing at 5 Mid Street, Pathhead, Kirkcaldy, on 9 November 1881 at Markinch Parish Church of Scotland. The wedding was conducted by Rev J L Rose, minister of Markinch; the best man was Thomas Law and the best maid was Ann Skinner.

William and Catherine had two known sons in Kirkcaldy; David (b. ~1883) and Annan Buchan (b. 5 May 1892) at 37 Victoria Road, Kirkcaldy. On 23 September 1891, William had to register the death of his father David Ness and just four years later, William was involved in a fatal accident at work. William Ness, only 34, a floor-cloth traveller, residing at Brown's Close, Bridgeton, Kirkcaldy, died on 5 October 1895 in the Cottage Hospital, Sinclairtown, Dysart of a rupture of the abdominal viscera, for 1 day, as a result of an accident as certified by Dr A L Curror MB CM. The death was registered by William's father-in-law John Blyth, of 12 Nethergate, Kinghorn on 7 October 1895 at the Dysart Registry Office.

In a Register of Corrected Entries, William Ness, 36, described curiously as a cement mixer, died as '*the result of being crushed between the framework of a hoist & the second floor in the factory of Fife Linoleum and Floorcloth Company (Limited) Kirkcaldy, as per verdict of jury. Survived about 4 hours as certified by Dr Curror, Kirkcaldy.*' The RCE was certified by R H Renton, Procurator Fiscal, on 9 November

1895 in Cupar. Catherine Ramsay Ness nee Blyth, 81, never remarried and died fifty years later in 1945 in Kirkcaldy.

Annan's paternal grandparents - David Ness and Jane Forrester

Annan's paternal grandfather David Ness was born around 1828 to father William Ness, a hand loom weaver, and mother Helen Seath, and his grandmother Jane Forrester, aka Jean, was born around 1832 to father Andrew Forrester, both in Dysart, Fife. David Ness, a weaver, married Jane Forrester on 9 September 1854 in Dysart. The marriage is recorded in the OPRs for the parish of Dysart (Ref: 427/7/303) as follows:-

1854: 9th September: David Ness, Weaver son of William N. and Jane Forrester, daughter of Andrew F., both of this parish, were contracted, and after proclamation married: Ness & Forrester

David and Jane had four known children in Dysart; Margaret (b. ~1855), Helen (b. ~1858), William (b. 27 December 1859) and Joan (b. ~1862). Son William Ness was born on 27 December 1859 at Sinclairtown, Dysart. In 1871, David Ness, 43, an unemployed linen weaver, resided at North Side High Street, Linktown, Kirkcaldy, with wife Jane, 39, a millworker, children Margaret, 16, and Helen, 13, both millworkers, William, 11, and Joan, 9, both scholars.

David Ness, 64, a floor-cloth worker, died on 23 September 1891 at 39 Victoria Road, Kirkcaldy of hepatitis, for 10 days, and pneumonia, for 7 days, as certified by Dr J

Sutherland Mackay MD. The death was registered by David's son William Ness on 23 September 1891 at the Kirkcaldy Registry Office. Jane remarried a second husband surnamed Beveridge and Jane Beveridge previously Ness nee Forrester was still alive in 1895.

Annan's maternal grandparents – John Blyth and Janet Fyfe

Annan's maternal grandfather John Blyth was born about 1839 in Thornton, Markinch, Fife to father Thomas Blyth, a miner, and mother Catherine Ramsay. In 1841, John, 2, resided in his grandmother Ann Ramsay's home in Thornton, Markinch, with his father Thomas Blyth, 35, a coal miner, mother Catherine, 25, and sister Ann, 3. Annan's grandmother Janet Fyfe (or Fyffe) was born illegitimately about 1842 in Fife to father James Fyfe, a tenter, and mother Christian Hoy.

John Blyth, 23, an iron moulder, of Markinch, married Janet Fyfe, 21, of Leslie, on 25 September 1863 in Markinch Parish Church of Scotland. The wedding was conducted by Rev J L Rose, minister of Markinch; the best man was William Blyth, John's brother, and the best maid was Agnes Buchan. Daughter Catherine Ramsay Blyth, who was also married later in Markinch by Rev J L Rose, was born on 19 February 1864 at Harbour Head, Kirkcaldy, Fife.

John Blyth, moulder in an iron foundry, and wife Janet were both still alive in Kirkcaldy in 1881. John, of 12 Nethergate, Kinghorn, registered the death of his son-in-law William Ness on 7 October 1895 at the Dysart Registry Office.

Annan's paternal great-grandparents - William Ness and Helen Seath

Annan's paternal great-grandfather William Ness and great-grandmother Helen Seath were both likely born around 1805 in Fife. William Ness, a hand loom weaver, married Helen Seath and they had a son David (b. ~1828) in Markinch. William, a hand loom weaver, and Helen were both dead by 1891.

Annan's paternal great-grandfather – Andrew Forrester

Annan's other paternal great-grandfather Andrew Forrester was possibly born around 1805 in Fife. Andrew Forrester may have married a wife named Margaret and they had a daughter Jane, aka Jean (b. ~1832) in Markinch. Andrew Forrester was still alive in 1854.

Annan's maternal great-grandparents – Thomas Blyth and Catherine Ramsay

Annan's maternal great-grandfather Thomas Blyth was born about 1806 and his great-grandmother Catherine Ramsay, aka Katherine, was born about 1816 to mother Ann Ramsay, both in Markinch, Fife. Thomas Blyth, a coal miner, married Catherine Ramsay and they had three known children in Thornton,

Markinch; Ann (b. ~1838), John (b. ~1839) and William (b. >1841). In 1841, Thomas Blyth, 35, a coal miner, resided in Thornton village, Markinch, with wife Catherine, 25, daughter Ann, 3, and John, 2. They were staying at the home of Catherine's widowed mother Ann Ramsay, 42, a woman of independent means. Thomas, a miner, was dead by 1863, although, his wife Catherine was still alive then and working as a shopkeeper.

Annan's maternal great-grandparents – James Fyfe and Christian Hoy

Annan's other maternal great-grandfather James Fyfe (or Fyffe) and his great-grandmother Christian Hoy were born about 1815 in Fife. James Fyfe, a tenter, an old Scots occupational name for a power loom mechanic, and Christian Hoy had a daughter Janet born illegitimately about 1842 in Fife. James Fyfe, a tenter, and Christian Hoy, who never married, were both still alive in 1863.

Annan's maternal great-great-grandmother – Ann Ramsay

Annan's maternal great-great-grandmother Ann Ramsay (her married name) was born about 1799 in Markinch, Fife. Ann married a husband surnamed Ramsay and they had two known daughters Catherine (b. ~1816) and Janet (b. ~1821) in Markinch. Ann was a widow of independent means, usually meaning her husband left her a pension or annuity to live on. In 1841, Ann Ramsay, 42, an independent, resided in Thornton, Markinch, with son-in-law Alexander Welch, 20, a stone miner, daughter Janet Welch, 20, another son-in-law Thomas Blyth, 35, a coal miner, daughter Catherine Blyth, 25, granddaughter Ann, 3, and grandson John, 2.

Chapter 15

Bob Preston
Private,
16th Battalion Royal Scots

Bob Preston (1895 – 1945)

Robert Malcolm Preston was born on 15 July 1895 at Whitelands, Loanhead, Lasswade, Midlothian, to father Thomas Preston, a shale miner, and mother Janet Malcolm. Around 1900, the Preston family moved to Kirkcaldy, Fife, but a few years later they moved to Bathgate, West Lothian. In 1911, Robert, 15, a coal miner drawer, resided at 61 Mid Street, Bathgate, with his father Thomas Preston, 40, a coal miner hewer, mother Janet, 42, and his other siblings. Known as Bob, he was a professional footballer who played at wing-half and centre-half for Hearts and later for English League clubs Plymouth Argyle and Torquay United. Preston signed for Hearts from Central League side Bathgate FC shortly before the outbreak of the war in 1914.

Bob's elder brother Thomas Preston (b. 1893, Loanhead) was a right-half, playing his entire professional career for Airdrieonians (1921–1932), having previously played for amateur side Loanhead Mayflower. Tom famously won the Scottish Cup with the Diamonds in 1924 with victory over Hibernian, Airdrieonians only senior trophy win. Tom was also selected for the Scottish League XI in 1924 and played in a triallist international game the following year for Scotland.

On 25 November 1914, Preston was among the Hearts players who volunteered to enlist in Sir George McCrae's new battalion of the Royal Scots. On 18 June 1915, as the battalion entrained for Studley Camp in Ripon, Preston was in hospital with influenza. On 24 October 1915, while still billeted in McCrae's reserve company at Heriot's School, Robert Preston, 22, a professional footballer and Private in the Royal Scots, married Violet Paley, 20, a musician, of 1 Panmure Place, Tollcross, Edinburgh, in a civil ceremony by warrant of the Sheriff Substitute for the Lothians and Peebles. Violet was the daughter of deceased father Joseph Paley, a draper, and mother May Audrey.

Military service soon took Preston away from Violet and Edinburgh for four long years, and it was 1919 before he made his debut for Hearts. He remained with the club until the 1922–23 season, making 127 appearances. He then transferred to Torquay United, playing in the Southern League, but quickly moved on to Third Division South club Plymouth Argyle in 1923. He made 143 appearances for the club in all competitions and his last game for Argyle came at the end of the 1927–28 season. He returned to Torquay United, by then a Football League team, for the following season in 1928–29, making 15 appearances.

After retiring from playing, Preston moved to Ireland and became a publican, also managing Sligo Rovers for one season in 1934–35. On 28 June 1934, Preston took former Showgrounds Junior side Sligo Rovers into the Irish Free State League, now the Football Association of Ireland. Their first FAI game was a 3–1 defeat against Dublin side St James Gate at the Iveagh Grounds. However, Preston managed Sligo to a creditable third place in the league with his forward Gerry McDaid ending up as the season's top scorer. Robert Preston, only 49, died in Northern Ireland in 1945, another Hearts man falling to the 'curse of the old 16th'.

Bob's parents -
Thomas Preston and Janet Watt Malcolm

Bob's father Thomas Preston was born on 4 January 1871 at Yorkston Farm, Temple, Midlothian to father Robert Preston, a ploughman, and mother Emily Samuel. The birth was registered by Thomas's father Robert Preston on 24 January 1871 at Temple Registry Office. Yorkston Farm, with associated structures, in the parish of Temple, is a Category B Listed Building.

The parish of Temple, also known in ancient times as Balantrodach, from the Gaelic meaning 'town of the warriors', is an ancient parish, once part of the lands owned by the fabled Knights Templar. It has close connections to nearby Roslin Chapel, which was also a Knights Templar stronghold in the Lothians, made famous by Dan Brown's novel *The Da Vinci Code*. Legend has it that treasure of the Knights Templar was removed secretly from Paris, to be hidden in Temple.

A local legend states: 'Twixt the oak and the elm tree, ye will find buried the millions free.' French legends about the Templar treasure apparently also state that it was taken to

Scotland, where the knights landed on the Isle of May, and the first island they encountered in the Firth of Forth. Geographically, this would take them to the mouth of the river Esk, leading them to Rosslyn (Roslin). Dan Brown fictionalised this mediaeval legend to suggest the treasure at Roslin Chapel was *The Holy Grail.*

Bob's mother Janet Watt Malcolm was born on 20 December 1868 at Camptoun, Haddington, Haddingtonshire to father Robert Malcolm, a ploughman, and mother Janet Watt. The birth was registered by Janet's father Robert Malcolm on 4 January 1869 at Haddington Registry Office. Camptoun, also once known as Captainhead, was an estate owned by the Earl of Wemyss, and Camptoun House, occupied by a Mr Skirving in the mid-19th century, is another Category B Listed Building and is now a boutique B&B hotel.

In 1871, Janet, 2, resided at Old Post Road, Amisfield Mains, Haddington, with her parents and siblings. When Janet left school she worked in the St Anne's Carpet Factory, a converted brewery, in Lasswade, Midlothian. In 1881, Thomas, 10, a scholar, resided at Old Lasswade Road, Edgehead, Liberton, with his father Robert Preston, 54, a farm servant, mother Emily, 45, a farm servant's wife, and siblings.

Thomas Preston, 22, a shale miner, of Oakbank, Liberton, married Janet Watt Malcolm, 24, a carpet factory worker, of Whitelands, Loanhead, on 6 October 1893. The wedding was conducted by Rev Alexander Stewart, minister of Loanhead Parish Church of Scotland; the best man was David Johnstone and the best maid was Rachael Malcolm, Thomas's younger sister. Thomas and Janet had four known children; in Loanhead, Thomas (b. 1893), Robert (15 July 1895), Harry (b. ~1898), and in Kirkcaldy, Nellie (b. ~1901). Son Robert Preston was born on 15 July 1895 at Whitelands, Loanhead, Lasswade.

In 1901 the Preston family lived in Kirkcaldy, however, by 1911, Thomas Preston, 40, a coal miner hewer, resided at 61 Mid Street, Bathgate, East Lothian, with wife Janet, 42, children Thomas, 17, a coal miner hewer, Robert, 15, a coal miner drawer, Harry, 13, and Nellie, 10, both at school. Also boarding at Thomas's home was his brother-in-law George Malcolm, 50, a coal miner hewer. Thomas, a coal miner, and Janet were both still living in Bathgate in 1915.

Bob's paternal grandparents -
Robert Preston and Emily Samuel

Bob's paternal grandfather Robert Preston was born around 1829 in Liberton, Midlothian to father James Preston, a ploughman, and mother Euphemia Snodgrass. His grandmother Emily Samuel was born on 6 October 1834 at Newlands, Peeblesshire to father Robert Samuel, a road surfaceman, and mother Elizabeth Tait. The birth is recorded in the OPRs for the parish of Newlands (Ref: 767/3/56) as follows:-

> *1834: Samuel: Emily Daughter of Robert Samuel and of his spouse Elizabeth Tait born 6th October*

Robert Preston, a ploughman, married first wife Jane Noble, daughter of George Noble, a coal agent, and his wife

Margaret. Jane Preston nee Noble, only 28, died on 13 July 1863 at Dalwick Mill, Stobo of bronchitis and peritonitis, for about a week, as certified by Alexander Kells, surgeon, Biggar. Robert Preston, widower, registered Jane's death on 23 July 1863 at the Stobo Registry Office.

Robert Preston, 36, a widowed ploughman, of Stoneyknowe, Newlands, married second wife Emily Samuel, 29, a domestic servant, of Stobo Mill, parish of Stobo, on 2 June 1865 at Newlands Mains farm. The wedding was conducted by Rev James Charteris, minister of Newlands Church of Scotland; the witnesses were John Tait, Elizabeth's brother, and David Moffat. The Reverend James Charteris was ordained in Newlands Old Church in 1834 and served his ministry in the New Church. Charteris was a Cadet of the influential Wemyss family, who currently still own estates in Peeblesshire.

Robert and Emily had eight known children; James (b. ~1867, Newlands), Robert (b. ~1868, Lasswade), Thomas (b. 4 January 1871, Temple), William (b. ~1873, Temple), Richard (b. ~1874, Stow), John (b. ~1875, Crichton), Euphemia (b. ~1877, Liberton) and Rachael (b. >1881). Son Thomas Preston was born on 4 January 1871 at Yorkston Farm, Temple, Midlothian. In 1881, Robert Preston, 54, a farm servant, resided at Old Lasswade Road, Edgehead, Liberton, with Emily, 45, a farm servant's wife, children James, 14, a farm servant, Robert, 13, Thomas, 10, William, 8, Richard, 7, John, 6, all scholars, and Euphemia, 4.

The village of Edgehead, also known as Chesterhill, in Midlothian was historically situated on the long straight Roman road known as Dere Street. The origin of the Roman name is obscured in time, but it may have been *Strada Derventio*, after the River Derwent and the Roman settlement at Malton called Derventio. Dere Street ran north from Eboracum (York) to Derventio (Malton), then Corbridge, through the Portgate on Hadrian's Wall, across Soutra Hill in the Lammermuirs, through Chesterhill, on to the Brittonic stronghold of Din Eidyn (Edinburgh), and terminating at the Roman fort on Antonine's Wall near Carriden, West Lothian.

Robert Preston, an oil work fireman, was still alive in 1893, although, his wife Emily was dead by then.

Bob's maternal grandparents -
Robert Malcolm and Janet Watt

Bob's maternal grandfather Robert Malcolm was probably born illegitimately around 1837 in Crichton, Midlothian to father George Malcolm, a gardener, and mother Janet Baillie. His maternal grandmother Janet Watt was also probably born illegitimately around 1838 in Athelstaneford, Haddingtonshire to father Richard Watt, a shepherd, and mother Elizabeth McKenzie.

Robert Malcolm, 22, a labourer, of Stevenson Lodge, Haddington, married Janet Watt, 21, of Abbey Mains, Haddington, on 10 June 1859. The wedding was conducted by Rev John Cook DD, minister of Haddington Church of Scotland; the witnesses were James Malcolm, Robert's brother, and James Watt, Janet's brother. Robert and Janet had five known children; in Garvald, George (b. ~1861),

Richard (b. ~1863), Robert (b. ~1865), in Humbie, Elizabeth (b. ~1867) and in Haddington, Janet (b. 20 December 1868). Daughter Janet Watt Malcolm was born on 20 December 1868 at Camptoun, Haddington.

In 1871, Robert Malcolm, 33, an agricultural labourer, resided at East Post Road, Amisfield Mains, Haddington, with wife Janet, 32, George, 10, Richard, 8, Robert, 6, all scholars, Elizabeth, 4, and Janet, 2. Robert, working as a gasman, and his wife Janet were both still alive in 1893.

Bob's paternal great-grandparents -
James Preston and Euphemia Snodgrass

Bob's paternal great-grandfather James Preston, the son of James Preston senior, and great-grandmother Euphemia Snodgrass were both born in Midlothian about 1800. James and Euphemia had two known sons in Liberton; Richard (b. 10 October 1826) and Robert (b. ~1829). Robert's birth record has not been found, however, Richard's birth is recorded in the OPRs for the parish of Liberton (Ref: 693/8/52) as follows:-

> *1826: Preston: Richard son to James Preston and*
> *Euphemia Snodgrass at ~~Cowslip~~ ^ Cowland ^ was born*
> *10th October and baptized 19th November 1826*
> *Witnesses James Preston Senior and William Steadman*

Son Robert Preston was born around 1829 in Liberton, Midlothian to father James Preston, a ploughman, and mother Euphemia Snodgrass. James, a ploughman, and Euphemia were both dead by 1865.

Bob's paternal great-grandparents – Robert Samuel and Elizabeth Tait

Bob's other paternal great-grandfather Robert Samuel and great-grandmother Elizabeth Tait were both born around 1805 in Dumfriesshire.

Robert, a road surfaceman, and Elizabeth had two known children; son John and daughter Emily (b. 6 October 1834) at Newlands, Peeblesshire. The birth is recorded in the OPRs for the parish of Newlands (Ref: 767/3/56) as follows:-

1834: Samuel: Emily Daughter of Robert Samuel and of his spouse Elizabeth Tait born 6th October

Robert, a road surfaceman, and his wife Elizabeth were both still alive in 1865.

Bob's maternal great-grandparents – George Malcolm and Janet Baillie

Bob's maternal great-grandfather George Malcolm and great-grandmother Janet Baillie were both born around 1810 in Midlothian. George Malcolm, a gardener, and Janet Baillie had a son Robert Malcolm probably born illegitimately around 1837 in Crichton, Midlothian. George Malcolm, a gardener, and Janet Baillie were both still alive in 1859.

Bob's maternal great-grandparents –
Richard Watt and Elizabeth McKenzie

Bob's other maternal great-grandfather Richard Watt and great-grandmother Elizabeth McKenzie were both born around 1810 in Haddingtonshire. Richard Watt, a shepherd, and Elizabeth McKenzie had a daughter Janet Watt probably born illegitimately around 1838 in Athelstaneford, Haddingtonshire. Richard, a shepherd, and Elizabeth McKenzie were both still alive in 1859.

Bob's paternal great-great-grandfather - James Preston

Bob's paternal great-great-grandfather James Preston was born around 1775 probably in Midlothian. James Preston senior had a son James Preston junior born in Midlothian about 1800. James Preston senior was still alive and a witness at his grandson Richard Preston's baptism on 19 November 1826 in Liberton, Midlothian.

Chapter 16

Willie Wilson
Private 62883,
16th Battalion Royal Scots

William Wilson (1894 – 1956)

William Rose Wilson was born on 28 February 1894 at 3 McLeod Street, Gorgie, Edinburgh, to father Robert Wilson, a foreman mason, and mother Margaret Rose. He was initially raised at McLeod Street, in the shadow of Tynecastle and he was a Hearts supporter from childhood. In 1901, William, 6, a scholar, resided at 265 Gorgie Road, Gorgie, Edinburgh, with his father Robert Wilson, 46, a foreman mason, mother Margaret R, 42, and his other siblings.

Wilson's father died in 1907 and in 1911, William, 17, an apprentice tinsmith in a meter factory, resided at 18 Ogilvie Terrace, Merchiston, Edinburgh, with his widowed mother Margaret Wilson, 51, a housekeeper, and his other siblings. William, a tinsmith, along with siblings James, Margaret and Isabella worked at the New Grange Works, Alder & Mackay's pre-paid gas meter manufactory in Stewart Street, Edinburgh.

Willie was a professional footballer, who played at outside left with Hearts. He began his career with local juvenile sides before joining Junior team Arniston Rangers in 1911–12, representing Scotland Juniors at that level in two matches. He was signed by McCartney in 1912, aged 18, alongside friend Paddy Crossan, a lodger at the Wilson family home. Wilson made his debut in April 1912 in a 2–0 defeat to Airdrieonians. In the following season, his tally in the league was an impressive 15 goals from 23 games as the club finished 4th. He continued to feature regularly for Hearts in 1913–14 when they finished 4th again, and at the outset of season 1914–15, they began strongly and were top of the league in November. By that point, the war was intensifying, and there followed a public and political backlash over the willingness of sportsmen to join up for the armed forces.

Eleven of the Hearts first and second squads, including Willie, enlisted en-masse on 25 November 1914 into McCrae's Battalion. The Scottish League continued to operate, but Hearts were depleted and they were beaten by Celtic into the runners-up spot. Wilson was selected for the Scottish League XI in March 1915. On 29 July 1916, as the Somme ended its first dreadful month of slaughter, Willie Wilson was the best man at Ernie Ellis's wedding in Edinburgh.

In 1915–16 military commitments began to take hold, and soon after scoring a hat-trick in a 4–0 away win over Rangers, Wilson was called up to join his unit. From then on he made occasional appearances for Hearts and, while at Ripon, he also had a spell as a guest player for Leeds City. In May 1916, he was selected for Scotland in a unique unofficial wartime international, alongside teammate Jimmy Frew.

While several of his teammates fought and perished at the Somme, a problematic dislocated shoulder, sustained on the football field rather than the battlefield, meant Wilson could not fire a rifle effectively, and he was held back in the

Royal Scots reserve company. He saw frontline action in April 1917 at the Battle of Arras (9 April–16 May 1917), but his shoulder injury turned out to be a blessing in disguise. The recoil of his rifle tended to dislocate it and two weeks at the front ended with a dislocated shoulder, trench fever and transfer home back into reserve. Private 62883 William R Wilson was awarded the Victory and British War medals.

After hostilities ended in 1918, Wilson returned to Edinburgh and played for Hearts in the 1919 Victory Cup final. For the next four seasons, he was an important component of the team, averaging 34 league games and 6 goals each campaign despite being troubled by his shoulder injury. William R Wilson, 25, a sheet metal worker, of 10 Ogilvie Terrace, Merchiston, Edinburgh, married Jeannie M Bryson, 19, a confectioner's assistant. In July 1923, he received a benefit match and a few weeks later left the club having amassed 273 competitive appearances, scoring 72 goals for Hearts.

Willie moved to second division club Cowdenbeath and in his first season helped them to gain promotion. His top-level career continued, as Cowdenbeath achieved an all-time high league placing of 5th in 1924–25 and were still in the First Division in Wilson's final season of 1928–29. He made 197 appearances for Cowdenbeath, scoring 37 goals. After retiring from football, Wilson ran a sweet shop with his wife Jeannie in Bristo, Edinburgh, and then he relocated to Stretford in Manchester to work in his trade as a tinsmith. William Rose Wilson, only 62, died in 1956 in Cheshire, shortly after his beloved Hearts lifted the Scottish Cup.

Willie's parents - Robert Wilson and Margaret Rose

Willie's father Robert Wilson was born illegitimately around 1854 in Haddington, Haddingtonshire to father Robert Wilson, a labourer, and mother Christian Storey, aka Elizabeth. Robert's parents married in 1857 in Haddington. His mother Margaret Rose, aka Maggie was born around 1855 in Mull, Argyllshire to father Alexander Rose, a farmer, and mother Catherine Cameron. In 1861, Robert, 6, a scholar, resided at West Port, Dunbar, with his father Robert Wilson, 26, a labourer, mother Christian, 28, and his brother James, 3. In 1871, Robert, 15, an apprentice mason, resided at Letham Toll House, Haddington, with his father Robert Wilson, 36, a road labourer, mother Christina, 38, and his brother James, 13, a scholar.

Robert Wilson, 24, a mason journeyman, married Maggie Rose, 23, a domestic servant, both residing at 24 Caledonian Crescent, St George, Edinburgh, on 10 December 1878. The wedding was conducted by Rev James Barclay; the best man was John Gilchrist and the best maid was Mary Campbell. Robert and Maggie had seven known children in Edinburgh; Catherine (b. ~1880), Christina (b. ~1884), Robert (b. ~1886), Margaret (b. ~1888), Isabella (b. ~1890), James (b. ~1893) and William Rose (b. 28 February 1894). Son William Rose Wilson was born on 28 February 1894 at 3 McLeod Street, Gorgie, Edinburgh.

In 1901, Robert Wilson, 46, a foreman mason, resided at 265 Gorgie Road, Gorgie, Edinburgh, with wife Margaret R, 42, Catherine, 21, a dressmaker on her own account, Christina, 17, a clerkess, Robert, 15, a van boy, and Margaret,

13, Isabella, 10, James, 8, William, 6, all four scholars. Robert Wilson, only 52, a mason, died on 2 September 1907 at 24 Slateford Road, Morningside, Edinburgh of chronic disease of the heart and mitral valve and a cerebral embolism as certified by Dr William Bannerman MD. The death was registered by his son Robert Wilson on 3 September 1907 at the Edinburgh Registry Office.

In 1911, Margaret Wilson, 51, a widowed housekeeper, resided at 18 Ogilvie Terrace, Merchiston, Edinburgh, with children Catherine, 31, a baker's shopkeeper, Robert, 25, a general labourer in a rubber factory, Margaret, 23, Isabella, 21, both meter workers in a meter factory, James, 18, and William, 17, both apprentice tinsmiths in the meter factory. Margaret Wilson, 62, died on 15 November 1922 at 10 Ogilvie Terrace, Morningside, Edinburgh, of malignant disease of the colon and intestinal obstruction as certified by Dr William Bannerman MD. The death was registered by her son Robert Wilson on 15 November 1922 at the Edinburgh Registry Office.

Willie's paternal grandparents - Robert Wilson and Christian Storey

Willie's paternal grandfather Robert Wilson was born around 1835 at Oldhamstocks, Haddingtonshire and his grandmother Christian Storey (or Storie), aka Elizabeth, was christened on 23 September 1832 at Gladsmuir, Haddingtonshire to father Alexander Storie and mother Jean Knowes. In 1851, Christian Storie, 19, a maid servant, resided at

Samuelston, Gladsmuir, at the home of Grace Brown, 83, a pauper. Robert Wilson, a labourer, married Christian Storey on 17 October 1857 in Haddington and they had two known sons; Robert (b. ~1854, illegitimate) in Haddington, Haddingtonshire and James (b. ~1858) in Dunbar, Haddingtonshire.

In 1861, Robert Wilson, 26, resided at West Port, Dunbar, with wife Christian, 28, sons Robert, 6, a scholar, and James, 3. In 1871, Robert Wilson, 36, a road labourer, resided at Letham Toll House, Haddington, with wife Christina, 38, sons Robert, 15, an apprentice mason, and James, 13, a scholar. Robert Wilson, a joiner, and his wife Christina were both dead by 1907.

Willie's maternal grandparents – Alexander Rose and Catherine Cameron

Willie's maternal grandfather Alexander Rose and his grandmother Catherine Cameron were born around 1835 probably in Mull, Argyllshire. Alexander Rose, a farmer, married Catherine Cameron and they had a daughter Margaret (b. ~1855) in Mull. Alexander, a farmer, and Catherine were still alive in 1878, however, they were both dead by 1922.

Willie's paternal great-grandparents – Alexander Storie and Jean Knowes

Willie's paternal great-grandfather Alexander Storie (or Storrie or Storey) and his great-grandmother Jean Knowes (or Knowis or Knows) were born around 1806 probably in

East Lothian. Alexander, a miller, and Jean married in Duddingston around 1825 and they had seven known children; in Duddingston, Elizabeth (b. 19 March 1826), in Gladsmuir; Janet (b. 20 July 1828), Alexander (b. 3 March 1831, died in infancy), Christian, aka Elizabeth (b. 23 September 1832), Alexander (b. 7 October 1834, died in infancy), Mary (b. 8 January 1837) and Alexander (b. ~1851).

Jean Storie nee Knowes was dead before 1871. At that time, Alexander Storrie, 65, a widowed miller, resided at West Derby, Lancashire, with daughter Mary, 34, and son Alexander, 20, a railway stoker.

Chapter 17

The other Hearts players on the
Roll of Honour who served in WW1

Although this book has concentrated on the 16 players who served in the 16th Royal Scots under Sir George McCrae, many other Hearts players and coaching staff served their country with honour and distinction during WW1.

John Allan, 9th Royal Scots
Killed in Action (KIA), 22 April 1917

Colin D Blackhall, 1st Lowland (City of Ed.)
Royal Garrison Artillery

James Gilbert, 1st Lowland (City of Ed.)
Royal Garrison Artillery

Harry N Graham, Gloucester Regiment and RAMC

Charles Hallwood, Royal Engineers

James Macdonald, 13th Royal Scots

John Mackenzie, 1st Lowland (City of Ed.)
Royal Garrison Artillery

Robert W Malcolm,
Royal Scots and Machine Gun Corps

John Martin, 5th Royal Scots,
twice wounded and discharged

Robert Mercer, 1st Lowland (City of Ed.)
Royal Garrison Artillery, gassed

George Miller, 9th Royal Scots, wounded

Neil Moreland, 8th HLI and 7th Royal Scots
wounded three times

George L Sinclair, Royal Field Artillery,
injured on service, discharged

James H Speedie, 7th Cameron Highlanders,
KIA, 25 September 1915

Philip Whyte, Gloucester Regiment

John Wilson, 9th Royal Scots, wounded in action twice

Also on the Hearts Roll of Honour

James Duckworth, Hearts trainer,
died of pneumonia, 25 August 1920

Alexander S Lyon, Hearts assistant,
died of influenza, 14 February 1915

Conclusion

First and foremost, this book is a commemoration of the lives of a group of young Heart of Midlothian players who answered the call to serve their country in the Great War. Too many of them made the ultimate sacrifice and laid down their lives on Flanders Field.

The family histories of these players wholly underline the humbleness of their ancestral origins. These were men and women who traversed Scotland, England, and Ireland to scratch out a meagre living as agricultural labourers, coal and shale miners, seamen, shipyard workers, linoleum workers, and domestic servants throughout the Dickensian Victorian era.

Into the 20th century, the family histories tell of the struggle to survive during the devastation of the Great War, the so-called, 'war to end all wars', and the sad losses incurred by so many families. It also details the dreaded 'curse of the old 16th', where the Hearts players who were not killed in action, had their lives cut short as an indirect consequence of the war.

In many ways, the family histories of these men and women are no different from our own family histories. Most of us can trace our ancestry back to humble beginnings throughout the agricultural and industrial revolutions. What defines this book is the culmination of these specific family histories in producing a group of remarkable young men. They put aside their sporting achievements and ambitions, and marched proudly along Princes Street with Sir George McCrae at the head of the 16th Battalion, the Royal Scots, the first 'sportsmen's battalion', and into the annals of history.

This book commemorates these extraordinary 'pals' of the Great War. The Pride of McCrae's and the Pride of Contalmaison. We salute them all.

Pride of the Hearts.

Hearts Player References

McCrae's Battalion, The Story of the 16th Royal Scots
Jack Alexander, 2003

Hearts at War: 1914–19, **Tom Purdie,** 2014

A Bigger Field Awaits Us: The Scottish Football Team That Fought the Great War, **Andrew Beaujon,** 2018

Genealogical References

National Records of Scotland, General Register House, Edinburgh

ScotlandsPeople.gov.uk

Association of Scottish Genealogists and
Researchers in Archives (ASGRA)

National Archives, Kew, London

Commonwealth War Graves Commission (CWGC)

FamilySearch.org

Ancestry.co.uk

Findmypast.co.uk

MyHeritage.com

Moray Council Local Heritage Centre

Cheshire Parish Registers

FreeBMD.org

FreeCEN.org

Online and Other References

The Mitchell Library

National Library of Scotland

ScotlandsPlaces.gov.uk

Canmore.org.uk

Londonhearts.org

Wikipedia.co.uk

Surname Database

Footballdatabase.eu

Fitbastats.com/Hearts

Edinburgh Evening News

The Scotsman

The Independent

Caledonian Mercury

Elgin Courant

Linlithgowshire Gazette

West Lothian Courier

Athletic News

Lancashire Evening Post

Football, Migration, and Industrial Patronage in the West of Scotland, c. 1870–1900, Sport in History, Matthew Lynn McDowell, 2012

Bell & Bain Ltd: Founded 1831, A Brief History © Bell & Bain Ltd, 2016

Ulster Medical Journal, 2008

Grace's Guide of British Industrial History

Scottishmining.co.uk

RailScot.co.uk

British Listed Buildings

Historic England

Kilbirnieheritage.com

Val McDermid, author, BBC Scotland News, Michael Sharkey, 2018

Pigot's Trade Directory, 1837

Happyhaggis.co.uk/Daphne.htm

Norwich-heritage.co.uk/shoe_factories

Sprowstonheritage.org.uk/Ellis_Family

THE PRIDE OF THE HEARTS

Glossary of Players' Origin of Surnames

Chapter 1: Boyd – a surname of Scottish origin generally believed to be a locational name based on the Isle of Bute, but may also be from the Gaelic 'buidhe' meaning yellow or fair-haired one.

Chapter 2: Currie – in Scotland this is generally a locational name from the village of Currie in Midlothian. It is believed to derive from the Gaelic 'curraigh' meaning a wet plain or marsh.

Chapter 3: Ellis – brought back by the Crusaders from the Holy Land, this surname derives from the Greek 'Elias' from the Hebrew 'Eliyahu' meaning Jehovah is God.

Chapter 4: Gracie – an ancient Scots Dalriada surname common in Argyllshire from the Gaelic 'greusaich' or 'griasaich', which originally meant an embroiderer, but eventually became a shoemaker.

Chapter 5: Hawthorn – an English locational surname believed to derive from the Old English 'haegporn' meaning 'thorn used for making hedges and enclosures' and believed, in Mediaeval times, to be one who resided within a hawthorn defensive enclosure.

Chapter 6: Wattie – a Scottish diminutive patronymic surname of Walter. Walter derives from the pre-7th century Frankish 'Waldhar' from 'wald' meaning to rule and 'hari' an army and introduced to Britain after the Norman Conquest.

Chapter 7: Briggs – this surname is a common variant of the English topographical surname Bridges and generally refers to one who lived beside a bridge, but could also be occupational for a bridge-keeper or maintainer.

Chapter 8: Crossan – an Irish surname from the pre-10ᵗʰ century Gaelic 'Mac an Croisan' meaning son of the young Cross and probably refers to someone who followed the Christian faith.

Chapter 9: Findlay – derived from the Gaelic personal name 'Fionnlagh' from the elements of 'finn' meaning white-haired and 'laoch' meaning a warrior or hero and probably derived from Norse-Viking origin.

Chapter 10: Frew – a Scottish locational surname derived from the Fords of Frew on the River Forth. Its origin is the pre-7ᵗʰ century Old English word 'frwd' meaning the lowest point of a river or stream, usually suitable as a crossing or ford.

Chapter 11: Hazeldean – an ancient Anglo-Saxon locational surname from the pre-7ᵗʰ century 'haesel' meaning hazel and 'denu' meaning a valley. In the case above the original locational surname in England was Hesselden, probably from Hesleden in County Durham.

Chapter 12: Low – as a Scottish surname, this most likely derives from the Old English pre-7ᵗʰ century topographical surname 'hlaw' meaning a hill or mound.

Chapter 13: McGuire – a notable Irish surname from the Gaelic 'Mac Uidhir' meaning son of the dun-coloured one.

Chapter 14: Ness – an ancient surname common in pre-7ᵗʰ century Gaelic, Old English and Norse-Viking from the topographical 'nes' meaning a headland or promontory.

Chapter 15: Preston – generally of English origin, this is a locational surname derived from any of the various places in England named Preston, most notably in Lancashire. It derives from the Old English pre-7th century 'preost' meaning a priest and 'tun' meaning an enclosed settlement.

Chapter 16: Wilson – one of the most common surnames in the British Isles, it is a diminutive patronymic surname meaning 'son of William'. Introduced into Britain by William the Conqueror it is a pre-8th century Frankish name from 'wil' meaning desire and 'helm' meaning a helmet or protection.

About the author

D erek Niven is a pseudonym used by the author John McGee, a member of ASGRA, in the publication of his factual genealogical writings and Derek Beaugarde for his fictional science fiction writings. John McGee, aka 'The Two Dereks', was born in 1956 in the railway village of Corkerhill, Glasgow and he attended Mosspark Primary and Allan Glen's schools. The late great actor Sir Dirk Bogarde spent two unhappy years at Allan Glen's when he was a pupil named Derek Niven van den Bogaerde, thus the observant reader will readily be able to discern the origin of the two pseudonyms. After spending 34 years in the rail industry in train planning and accountancy John McGee retired in 2007.

In 2012 the idea for his apocalyptic science fiction novel first emerged and *2084: The End of Days* © Derek Beaugarde was published by Corkerhill Press in 2016. This was followed by *Pride of the Lions* © Derek Niven published in 2017, *Pride of the Jocks* © Derek Niven, foreword by Kathleen Murdoch, published in 2018 and *Pride of the Bears* © Derek Niven published in 2020.

Three further books in the Pride Series are in the planning stages; *Pride of the Dons: the untold story of the men and women who made the 1984 Aberdeen ECWC winners* © Derek Niven, *Pride of the Three Lions: the untold story of the*

Available to buy from the same author

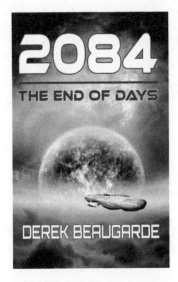

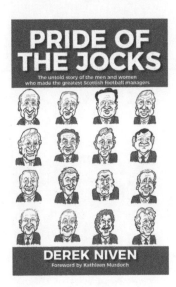

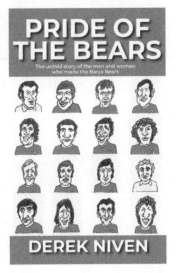

Lightning Source UK Ltd.
Milton Keynes UK
UKHW040719160322
400089UK00001B/53

9 780993 555183